HOW TO STAY MARRIED
& LOVE IT EVEN MORE!

Completing the Puzzle of a SoulMate Marriage

EVEN MORE continues the journey begun in How to Stay Married & Love It! by adding the remaining six pieces to the SoulMate puzzle.

Nancy Landrum, MA

How to Stay Married & Love It Even More! Completing the Puzzle of a SoulMate Marriage

Table of Contents

How to Stay Married & Love It Even More!

Completing the Puzzle of a SoulMate Marriage

Introduction

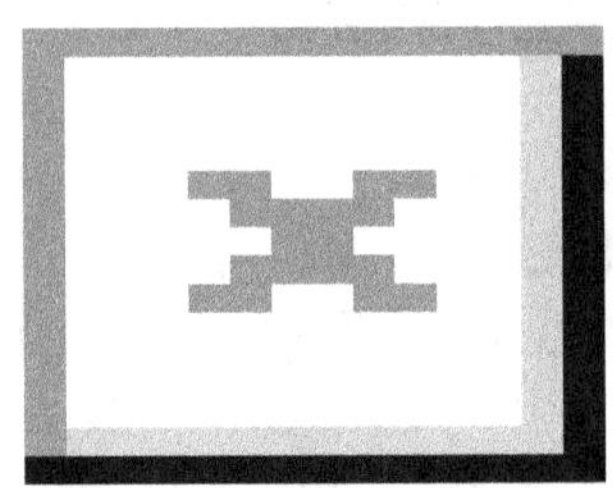

**"Love is what matters.
When all is said and done, love is what we remember.
On your deathbed you won't say 'I wish I'd made more money,
I wish I had worked more.'
You will grieve the lost opportunities for love,
and celebrate the ones you had."
Pat Love[1]**

When I start a jigsaw puzzle, I like to get the four corner pieces in place first. It defines the field, so to speak—letting me see the parameters within which the rest of the pieces will fit. In <u>How to Stay Married & Love It</u>! (from now on referred to as Book #1) we "framed" the puzzle of a SoulMate marriage by defining the four most essential elements. Those elements establish the dimensions and foundation for a SoulMate marriage.

---

[1] Love, Pat, Ed.D., 2001. The Truth About Love, p.243. New York: Fireside.

When I was eleven years old, my parents decided to build a new house. Up until then, the only home I had known was about 1200 square feet of squeaky hardwood floors, real plaster walls, wood framed windows and a little front porch. My two older sisters shared a small room. My younger sister and I shared a double bed in an even *smaller* room. All four of us shared a miniscule bathroom, the site of many squabbles.

The location of the new house was only about a mile away, so we visited the building site often. The first few weeks went by with very little observable progress. A tractor moved some dirt around. Sticks with red ribbons tied to them seemed to be randomly distributed over the area. Trenches were dug, big pipes laid and more pipes added. Some wires were strung about and hung from poles. It didn't look anything like a house to me. I wondered how the workmen knew what to do. It was a *huge puzzle*.

After several weeks of what appeared to be little change, I heard the excitement in my mother's voice when she said, "They're pouring concrete today!" I knew that meant a foundation. Maybe *now* it would start to look more like a house.

After the concrete hardened, we walked over the foundation as my mom described where the various rooms would be. I was afraid she'd made a big mistake. It looked so small. If we weren't going to have more room, why couldn't we stay in the old house that I loved? It was familiar. I was dreading the move. Mr. Dorming, the Swedish master-builder, assured me that the new house was considerably bigger than our current abode. Darn.

From that point on everything happened fast. It seemed that it became a real house overnight. The walls were framed in a blink. I could walk down a hallway, enter rooms and see where the long bathroom counter would go with two sinks and a huge mirror for my sisters and I. It was such a *long* walk from the back bedroom to the family room—how did the space become so big? The transformation felt like magic.

Since then I've explored many homes under construction. I've learned that the foundation *alone* appears deceptively small. Once the walls are framed, defining the various living areas, the true space of the house can be more accurately assessed.

When Jim and I were laying the foundation of our SoulMate marriage it seemed to take forever. It was tedious work. Progress was measured in inches. It was like a chaotic building site with trenches, pipes and wires randomly scattered about. The tools were unfamiliar and felt awkward to use. We knew that we *didn't* want to live in the old angry marriage anymore, but we had only a vague concept of what we were trying to build. The amount of work was daunting.

In addition, the dimensions of the foundation felt too small. The confines of *respectful* communication sometimes made me feel claustrophobic. Our agreement specifically barred sarcasm, yelling, attacking "you" statements and bringing up old business. Leaving in a huff, slamming doors, withdrawing in martyred silence and self-righteous accusations didn't fit within the parameters, either. Jim and I some times longed for the days when we said whatever we wanted to say without going through an internal check to see if the words and tone of voice conformed to our chosen limits.

It was only after our relationship continued to improve and expand that we began to appreciate what a magnificent foundation we had. A lovely, spacious marriage-home was gradually taking shape. My parents had Mr. Dorming to insure that all the important pieces fit and the foundation perfectly matched the plans. We believe there was a *Master Builder* at work in our marriage. Although we hadn't known *what* we needed or *how* to read the blueprints, all the essential pieces of the foundation for a great marriage were in place. In review, they are:

One: A SoulMate Point of View—Accept that you and your partner both have legitimate points of view.

Two: SoulMate Communication—Communicate in ways that facilitate hearing each other, creating greater intimacy and resolution of issues.

Three: SoulMate Respect—Always treat each other with respect and use anger to create deeper intimacy.

Four: SoulMate Commitment—Commit to this partner, this marriage, for life.

If you haven't read <u>How to Stay Married & Love It!</u> I urge you to put *this* book down and read *that* one first. The skills taught in Book #1 are foundational to the skills proposed in "Even More." The puzzle of a SoulMate marriage needs a clearly defined frame before the rest can be successfully completed.

As we learned to stay within the parameters of our marriage-foundation, we felt safe and secure. Our depleted energy resources were gradually restored. We gained confidence that we could live at peace and even joyfully with each other "'til death do us part." The remaining six pieces began falling into place to complete the multi-dimensional puzzle of a SoulMate marriage. Those are the qualities described in *How to Stay Married & Love It EVEN MORE! Completing the Puzzle of a SoulMate Marriage.*

Unlike cardboard puzzles, your marriage is a multi-dimensional puzzle—a living, breathing, changing organism. Every exchange—each separate act—influences the relationship in a negative or a positive way. A SoulMate marriage-house is built piece by piece, day by day, as the skills that express each of these ten qualities are practiced in relationship with your spouse.

Although not a physical house, this marriage structure provides shelter impossible for wood or stone to give. By putting into practice the skills recommended in Book #1 you've been framing the puzzle—building from scratch or shoring up your marriage foundation. We invite you to continue this exciting process. Add the next six pieces to *complete* the puzzle of a SoulMate marriage. As you do, your marriage becomes a shelter safely housing a place of intimate belonging and romantic loving for you and your spouse for life!

This volume begins with a concept that we took for granted in "How to #1," yet perhaps that was a mistake. The concept of choosing and living by our priorities is foundational to a SoulMate relationship! Read on...

"It is in the shelter of each other that the people live."
Irish Proverb

"There are three things to wonderful for me to understand—no, four!
How an eagle glides through the sky.
How a serpent crawls upon a rock.
How a ship finds its way across the heaving ocean.
The growth of love between a man and a woman."
Proverbs 30:18, 19[2]

---

[2] Unless otherwise noted, all Bible quotes are from The Living Bible by Tyndale House, available in most bookstores.

Puzzle Piece #5:

Put First Things First!

Chapter 1

Put First Things First

**"Marriage creates a situation in which our desire
to be served and coddled can be replaced
with a more noble desire to serve others."[3]**

Tad and Liz[4] had been working hard on their relationship and were making great progress. Then Tad told her about his deep desire to participate in a dangerous recreational activity. She was stunned. His participation in this activity would affect her life in ways she absolutely did not want! They were at a standoff. He agreed, reluctantly, to postpone any action until the issue was satisfactorily resolved between the two of them, but I could see the direction this was going. They were each marshaling their arguments for their respective positions. They were preparing for an appointment where I would hear each side and, like the judge on a television courtroom drama, decide which argument had the most merit. It was a no-win situation for all of us. One of them would "win" the battle but lose some ground in the building of a SoulMate relationship, the other one would "lose" and have ammunition for long-term resentment, and I. . . well I *knew* I would not place myself in the position of "judge."

While running errands I was thinking about the appointment I had with them later that day and wondering how to approach this issue so that everyone would win . . . a seeming impossibility, until I remembered how Lady, our beloved boxer dog, came into our lives.

---

[3] Thomas, Gary, (2000). <u>Sacred Marriage</u>, p. 186. Grand Rapids, MI: Zondervan.
[4] Fictitious names.

The boys and I were camping in the mountains of Northern California with extended family. We went to the nearby town one afternoon to do laundry. Peter, age 4, with his brother and cousins, wandered down the sidewalk to visit the pet shop. While waiting for the wash cycle to finish, I saw Peter weaving his way through the corridor between washers and dryers, dodging laundry baskets and women folding underwear. He had a little puppy pressed against his chest and a big wet spot on his shirt. His eyes were huge and pleading. "Mommy, can we take this puppy home?"

My heart sank. I didn't like dogs. When I was seven years old I got caught in the middle of a dogfight. My arm got in the way of snapping jaws. I still had the scars. After my husband died, I'd tried two different times to provide my boys with a dog—both times were disasters. I didn't want to try again. It was hard, however, to just say "No" to the longing in my son's eyes, so I gave him an answer that I thought was safe. "Peter, if you really want a dog, you will have to ask God to change my heart because right now, I don't want a dog, so my answer is no."

I knew my child. If he pestered about something constantly, it was relatively unimportant—a fleeting desire in his little heart. If he brought up a subject once in a great while, it was something that resided deeper within—something much more important to him. Every 4 to 6 months he would quietly approach me and ask, "Mommy, can we get a dog?" Each time I repeated my answer that I didn't like dogs, didn't want to take care of a dog, didn't want to get stuck with training, or cleaning up, or feeding a dog. I'd always soften the blow by adding, "If you really want a dog, you'll have to ask God to change my heart." Three years went by. Peter refined his dream. On the rare occasions when he would mention the subject, I heard that he now wanted a large dog with many colors and spots because dogs of only one color were "boring."

For reasons unimportant to this story, I decided to fence the back half of our quarter-acre lot. The morning after the chain link had been installed, I looked at the enclosed backyard. I was startled when this thought popped, unbidden, into my mind, "What a perfect place for a large dog!" Oh, no! I *couldn't* think that! I *don't* want a dog! I shrugged it off. Nevertheless, a strange thing began to happen. I spontaneously began to wake up at 5:30 a.m. every day *longing* for a dog! I'd lay in bed telling myself I was crazy and reciting all the reasons why I *didn't* want a dog! After 2 weeks of this aggravating routine, I took the boys to a pet shop to buy an aquarium and some gold fish in hopes that the acquisition would quell my dog impulses. While they were choosing fish, two fawn-colored boxer puppies reached out and grabbed my heart. I stifled my reaction so the boys wouldn't see. I paid for the fish and we left, but I couldn't exorcise those puppies from my mind. Even though they were monochromatic in color and had no spots, I *really wanted* one of those boxer puppies.

Finally I thought, "O.K. I give up. If one of those puppies is still there one week from today, I'll go back and get it," but after only three days, I couldn't wait any longer! While the boys were at school I drove to the pet shop. They were both gone! Both had been sold! I was heart-broken. I got in the car and, to my embarrassment, nearly cried. Part of me was *incredulously* watching this drama . . . what was *happening* to me? Didn't I know that as soon as we got a puppy home and it had an "accident" on the carpet or chewed up my favorite flowers I'd regret it? Even so, I couldn't seem to stop myself.

I went straight home from the pet store and opened the Yellow Pages. I found a boxer breeder who had puppies that were ready to be weaned. One of the puppies had poor conformation for a show dog so the breeder was willing to sell her as a pet. Although I wondered about the (assumed) "boring" color and no spots, the force that was behind this compulsion seemed to have honed in on boxers, so I went with it.

A nice lady opened the door to my knock. I barely greeted her before my attention was riveted on a puppy sitting quietly in the hallway behind her. I heard the breeder say that this was the one that was for sale. As I remember it, there were several other puppies in the room, but my internal radar zeroed in on only this one. As I approached her, I realized that she had *multi-colored* striated bands of fawn, brown, rust, chestnut, chocolate, and black—with a white belly, chest and collar around her neck. I had never heard of or noticed what the breeder called "brindle" coloring! By this time the puppy was in my arms, licking my face as though she had been waiting *forever*, and I had *finally* arrived. When I noticed a large *spot* of brindle color in the center of the white on the back of her neck, there was no question about it—*this* was the dog that Peter had dreamed and prayed into my heart! I adored her!

Tad and Liz made themselves comfortable in my office. Tad initiated discussion of "the issue." I interrupted him and asked permission to relay a story that had come to mind as I was thinking about their dilemma. They both agreed, so I told them the story of how Lady became a beloved member of our family. As I finished, I asked him if he would be willing to trust that either Liz would change her mind or his desire for the dangerous activity would disappear so that they could experience a win-win whichever way it went? To my surprise, he immediately said, "Yes. I can do that!"

Liz sat there stupefied. She'd come armed for battle. She said, "How'd you do that? I thought Tad would list his reasons for doing this and I'd list my reasons for not doing it . . . (just as I suspected) and I didn't know what would happen next! You just bypassed the whole argument!" This was one of those times when I know I am not alone in the counselor's chair. Either way, they both win!

My father and two of his brothers were partners in a vegetable-growing business for more than 40 years. In all that time they never fought. At the outset of their partnership they had agreed that all decisions would be unanimous. If one of them hesitated about a particular opportunity, all three of them would shelve it. Sometimes the reluctant one would change his mind in the coming weeks or months, and then, because they were now unanimous, they'd move forward.   Other times the two who had been gung-ho in the beginning, were later grateful that the third one had applied the brakes. The priorities of their relationships and the unity of their partnership were higher than any particular business decision. With this agreement, they may have missed a few good opportunities through the years, and they probably missed some disasters, as well, but for as long as they lived, they were good friends and trusted allies for each other.

When building and maintaining a great marriage is a high priority, other things find their proper place in your life. When the marriage is not a high priority, other things, even minor things, constantly whittle away at it.

For instance, issues about driving with a spouse are frequently brought up in our classes. Recently one young husband said that he often feels nagged about how he's driving. In his mind, his wife should only need to hear, "I'm sure I'm safely in control of the car" in order to be reassured and let the issue rest. His reassurance doesn't still her anxiety, however. He felt defensive and "right." She felt resentful and "right." I asked him what his reason was for driving fast. He answered that he believes in being on time—that it is an act of respect for whomever he is meeting. He already knew and usually practiced the typical time management tips such as: work backwards from the appointment time, subtract the time the journey may require, then, note the time to leave home, and so on. Sometimes, however, life happens and for whatever reason, he'd find himself short on time.

I said, "*Everyone* knows the car feels safer in the driver's seat than in the passenger seat! It's much harder to be on the side without a steering wheel or brake!" The class laughed in agreement. I asked, "What would your behavior be if you valued the respect and comfort of your wife more than the respect of the person with whom you have the appointment?" He instantly knew that he would slow down in honor of reducing her anxiety.

Jim and I used to have "driving" issues. We settled them forever the day we agreed that whoever is in the passenger seat rules. If he's driving and I need more space between our car and the car we're following, all I have to do is ask, "Would you leave more space?" and it's done immediately. If I'm driving and he's uncomfortable with the speed, he quietly says so and I immediately slow down. It's a matter of maintaining our *priority* of mutual respect.

In addition to pleasing him, graciously cooperating with Jim's request is a smart thing to do for myself—then *he* will be happy to give me the driving conditions *I* want when *I'm* in the passenger seat!

Every decision we make is based on our priorities. Priorities are not demonstrated by what we say, but by how we act—spend our time, energy, and money—how we speak, our tone of voice—*every* decision. I believe most of us would *say* that good health is a high priority, but, according to the national statistics, many of us suffer health conditions that are the result of poor eating, inadequate exercise, and careless life-style choices. Our *behaviors* expose our *real* priorities.

Every person I've ever asked has *said* that he or she wants a SoulMate relationship. Many of those same persons, however, continue to *choose* excessive working hours, say "yes" to many optional responsibilities, spend hours in front of the television, or persist in using communication tools that he or she *knows* are destructive. When the marriage gets only the leftovers of time, effort, or energy, its low priority is revealed.

On the first week of a recent workshop, one husband, after looking over the homework, said with an expression of surprise on his face, "It looks like this is going to take some time!" Yes! It requires time to take the car in for gas, washing, and regular servicing. It requires time to clean the house, or maintain a good relationship with business clients, or nurture a lovely yard, or invest in exercising for good health. Why should we expect a relationship as complex as marriage to flourish without the regular, scheduled attention we expect to give a car?

In our society there is monumental competition for our attention. The entire advertising industry tries to convince us that it is a high priority to purchase this product, buy that gizmo, or have a certain experience. Lately I've been thinking how very hard it is to keep my life simple. I think we must face at least 100 times more choices per day than the average person a century ago. Just walking into a grocery store brings me face to face with thousands of choices that I would not have had until recent years. I can't buy tires for the car, a new television set, or even a dress, without looking at the options and going through a process of elimination. Because of publications like "Consumers Digest," I tend to feel irresponsible and guilty if I buy something without researching all the pros and cons.

The complexities of contemporary life require that we work harder at consciously identifying and living according to our true priorities. Without *conscious* choices, various media, the pace of those around us, or the demands of a boss, a friend, or a family member, will use up our available energy on things that may not, ultimately, give us what we really desire.

After my father died, Mom instituted a practice that demonstrated something that was a very high priority for her—frequent contact with her family. She announced that she would be at a particular fast food restaurant each Wednesday at noon. Every member of the family who joined her at that time and place would have his or her lunch purchased by my mother (with her senior-citizen discount!). She insisted on being there even on days when she could barely walk or wasn't very hungry. For several years, her energy and money were spent on this priority. The group varied from 3 or 4 up to 20 persons, week after week.

Before they left our class last night, one couple registered for Workshop II. As they walked out the door they told us they hoped that, by the time they finished Workshop II next month, we'd have a III, and then a IV! They have been enjoying the evening set aside for the primary purpose of investing in their relationship. It's easier to maintain that priority when they've written out a check and are expected to show up each class night with their homework completed! I suggested that, perhaps, by the end of Workshop II, they might choose to maintain the habit of one evening a week devoted to their marriage. It will take conscious effort to keep that priority when there are so many other options vying for their attention.

Our priorities are enormously influenced by our beliefs.[5] One client's husband works until 9 or 10 o'clock two or three nights per week, and often on Saturday afternoon. It is this man's belief that he puts in long hours to provide adequately for his family, but his paycheck would be the same if he were home every evening at 5:30 p.m. and spent the entire weekend with his family. I suspect that he

---

[5] See Chapter 26, "The SoulMate Train."

unconsciously adopted his father's pattern of long work hours and low family involvement without ever examining the beliefs driving the behavior. This genuinely loving husband and father may have the belief that a man is responsible only if he works long hours. It is a high priority for him to be a responsible man, so he works long hours. He justifies it by saying that it's out of love for his family, but I have yet to hear of a family who, when the husband and father died, complained that he spent too much time with them. In order to choose behaviors that would be more supportive of a priority to meet his family's emotional needs, he may need to examine his belief about what defines a responsible man.

Tim and Sally[6] were engaged. Besides preparing for a lovely wedding, they decided to take our workshop as preparation for their marriage. When some troubling issues arose, they asked to see me privately. Sally had some communication habits that were very disturbing to Tim. He was not confident about following through with the wedding if Sally persisted in these behaviors. Sally mirrored Tim's feelings about this issue while I coached. When he felt heard, it was Sally's turn to speak. After apologizing for his hurt, and assuring him that she would diligently work on improving her behavior, she brought up a need of hers that had been consistently ignored by Tim. He heard her, but was becoming defensive. It eventually came to light that he believed his behavior (that prevented the meeting of her need) was just who he was—so he *couldn't* change to accommodate her, while her behavior was something she was *capable* of changing. You may be smiling, but Tim's belief is shared by many. It stems from a misperception of behaviors as the essence of *who we are* rather than *habits* that may need to be adjusted.

If my partner asks me to do something that is violating my sense of integrity, my morals, or is unsafe, my responsibility is to protect my alignment with my inner values and personal safety. If my partner has needs or desires that can be met if I am willing to change a habit, however, then the priority of a SoulMate relationship requires that I change a habit!

---

[6] Fictitious names.

I adopted many behavior patterns that originally served a valid purpose, but are not necessary to the genuine expression of who I am. Many of those behavior patterns became masks that prevented authentic expression of my true Self. As I have already mentioned, I used to be painfully shy. It served a good purpose at one time, but eventually became a barricade between me and the warm, friendly person I wanted to be. I have changed many of those behaviors, forcing myself outside my comfort zone (shyness) by initiating conversations and learning to ask questions. I changed the belief[7] behind the shy behaviors by choosing to believe that I am basically safe in the world, and will intuitively know if I need to protect myself. I made those changes in behavior and belief because I consciously chose a different priority—one of being more available to life and loving rather than the priority of hiding to keep myself safe. I am still an introvert by nature, but I am no longer shy and find myself getting to know and enjoying people far more than I did when I cloaked my true Self in shyness.

One of the peripheral benefits of making the journey toward a SoulMate relationship a high priority is that this path will faithfully and mercifully remove many of the "false faces" that hinder our experience of loving and being loved. Jim proved that a SoulMate relationship with me was a very high priority for him when he consented to see a counselor, refrained from hopeless talk, agreed to new family rules, and learned how to be more emotionally available to me—all behaviors that were initially very uncomfortable for him. I proved that a SoulMate relationship with him was a very high priority for me when I chose to vent anger safely, gave up the use of sarcasm, learned to stop myself from giving unwanted advice and reminded myself frequently to verbalize appreciation for Jim's many fine qualities—all behaviors that were very difficult for me to change.

And it's not over—this proving of our priorities. Every time he graciously extends the distance between our car and the one in front at my request; every time he requests a mirroring session when he has an issue; every time he checks with me before making plans; every time he expresses his love by opening a door for me, or writing a love note, or stopping on his way out the door to hug and kiss me; he's proving, again, that a SoulMate relationship with me is still a

---

[7] As described in Chapter 25, "The SoulMate Train."

very high priority for him. Every time I tell him how much I appreciate all the energy he devotes to supporting us; every time I praise his valuable contributions to the success of our workshops; every time I surrender to the slow seduction of his love-making; every time I tell him the truth about what I feel or need, I'm proving, again, that a SoulMate relationship with him is still a very high priority to me.

Are you willing to consciously examine and evaluate your priorities? Are you willing to look at your *behaviors* rather than trust your *words* about what is important to you? Are you courageous enough to ask your spouse and children what they see as your priorities? Will you look at the condition of your marriage, or the behavior of your children, and ask if they may be a reflection of your priorities?

Puzzle Piece #5: SoulMate love thrives when SoulMates put first things first!

Every day I re-evaluate my choices and make course corrections so my behaviors demonstrate my priority of a SoulMate marriage.

"We make a living by what we get, but we make a life by what we give."[8]

"One who doesn't give the gift (loving behaviors) he promised is like a cloud blowing over a desert without dropping rain."
Proverbs 25:14

---

[8] This quote is attributed to several different people (Winston Churchill, Norman Kennedy, MacEwan, and George Elliot to name a few). It's a great quote, but I don't know who said it first!

Puzzle Piece #6:

A SoulMate Vision

Chapter 2

Blueprint for a SoulMate Marriage

Jim had taken me to Laguna Beach to a surf-side restaurant for breakfast. The date was to discuss the pros and cons of a possible marriage between us. After breakfast, we decided to drive to a quiet spot on the beach for our discussion. As soon as we left the restaurant and got in the car, however, Jim put his arms around me and said, "I don't really care what we find out in this discussion. I want you to know that I want to marry you. Will you marry me?"

My heart leaped, but I still felt very hesitant. I asked if we could have our discussion first. He agreed. We aired our respective concerns within view of some of the most beautiful scenery in California. He reassured me that I would be *his* wife, not the church's (I was not thrilled about being a minister's wife), we discussed our children (three of whom were teenagers who would still live at home), we talked about our separate homes (where to live, whom to uproot), and a few other potential issues. In the end, it seemed like nothing was insurmountable, but I was still not able to give him a "yes." The responsibility of choosing what was best, not only for myself, but for my boys, was heavy on my heart.

Several days went by. Jim was patient; he told me that the absence of a "yes" was better than a definite "no." One evening he arrived early for a movie date. He sat on the piano bench while I ironed the clothes I planned to wear. He was asking if I wanted to see this movie, or that one. Finally I turned to him and said, "Do you remember the question you asked me the other day? The answer is 'yes!'"

He jumped up, let out a whoop that I'm sure the neighbors could hear, grabbed me, and danced me around the little workroom nearly upsetting the ironing board! Euphoria is the only word that describes our emotions that night.

A few days later his senior pastor and wife joined us for dinner at my house. I had set the table with a navy blue tablecloth and arranged a bouquet of white mums in a small pewter bowl to compliment my white dishes. We enjoyed a great dinner and "getting to know you" conversation. I cleared the table. When I came back, carrying dessert, there was a single diamond sparkling against the dark blue of the tablecloth! I wasn't really surprised by Jim's proposal of marriage, but I was flabbergasted by the gift of a diamond! I hadn't expected anything but a gold wedding band! While I was breathless and speechless, Jim said we'd take it in to choose a setting later that week. In spite of being a little self-conscious in front of the senior pastor, I jumped up to give Jim a big hug and a kiss! What other response can there possibly be to receiving such a beautiful, valuable, and unexpected confirmation of our betrothal?

A journey begins the moment the question is asked and answered, "Yes!" It is understood that the journey will lead to marriage, but first, a wedding must take place. It's the wedding, in most cases, that becomes the focus of attention. For some, bridal magazines are purchased, friends are consulted, bridal shows are attended, budgets discussed, wedding planners are interviewed, vendors are hired, and a date and time are chosen. For others, the choice is a simple ceremony in front of a judge or an elopement to Las Vegas. Either way, as ideas are examined and either chosen or discarded, a clearer image begins to emerge about what is wanted for the wedding. Every effort expended is for the purpose of bringing that inner image into outer, physical reality on the wedding day. Whichever images are chosen, the journey leads to a place on the life-map called "marriage."

From that place on the map, many directions can be taken. It never occurred to me to put any time, energy or thought into the ultimate destination of the marriage. I expected a good relationship to evolve just because we loved each other, but without a definite destination in mind, one may wander all over the map, visiting many undesirable locations.

I had a vague idea of what the evolution of our marriage would look like. I remember envisioning lots of great cuddling and sex; being proud to be seen with him; nudging the person next to me when he sang the national anthem at California Angels baseball games and saying, "He's my husband!"; being treated like a princess; working together in harmony; quietly talking out any differences that we might have; five children who would love and respect us; fun family vacations; romantic get-aways for two; and more money than I'd had before, as now there would be two sources of income! All of these expectations were vague, foggy images and none of them were shared with Jim! I simply assumed they would happen!

My dreamy images of marriage to Jim were similar to wanting a vacation on a tropical island. I pack a bathing suit and flip-flops, drive to the airport, randomly board a plane, and expect to land on a tropical island! I neglect to note that, from that particular airport, planes fly to Detroit, Hong Kong, and Vancouver, as well as Hawaii, Fiji, and St. Thomas. Even if I am lucky enough to board a plane heading for some tropical island, is it the one I want? Are the accommodations primitive or luxurious? Are golfing and snorkeling available or is it known primarily for its deep-sea fishing? Does it feature a wild-life preserve or is it known for its wild night life?

There have been four essential components to every successful journey I've ever taken, whether it's to the corner grocery store or Timbuktu:

Step 1. Point of Origin

The first necessary component is to know where you are now. Flying to Hawaii from Japan would require a very different route than flying to Hawaii from Los Angeles. First, "How to Stay Married & Love It!" and now this volume have given you the opportunity to assess where you are in your marriage in several different categories. Do you honor each other's points of view? What communication tools do you use? Are your communication tools helping you respectfully get the results you want? Is anger a resource for understanding or a weapon? What is the level of your commitment? Do your priorities need to be examined and rearranged? In later chapters you'll have the chance to ask: Do you speak your partner's love language? Are you making plenty of deposits into your Love Bank? Are you expressing appreciation whenever you can? Is there a barrier of resentment between you and your partner created by co-dependency? Do you have limiting beliefs that are hindering your progress to SoulMate love? Have you neglected romance?

Every marriage is always going somewhere! A relationship is never immobile. In your assessment, you may have determined that, currently, your relationship is in a location you never had any intention of being, similar to finding yourself in the Florida everglades when you'd planned to go skiing in Vale, Colorado. As Jim and I did, you may find yourself in a place of conflict, resentment, and distrust—or as others have, in a place of vague discontent. You may be teetering on the brink of a divorce when you planned to love and honor each other until parted by death.

Step 2. A Chosen Destination

I presume that you want the destination to be a SoulMate quality of relationship. I doubt you would have picked up this book, or read to this point, if your desire is for anything less than SoulMate love.

Step 3. Means of Travel and a Road Map

This book has provided many vehicles and specific roadways through which you might transport yourselves to the destination of SoulMate love, if you should choose to use them. All of the "roads" described in this book are tried and true and will speed you toward the destination of a SoulMate relationship. The specifics of how that would look and function is up to you and your partner.

4. Shelter upon Arrival

What will a SoulMate relationship look like for you? How will you know when you've arrived? There are couples who appear to me to have wonderful, even SoulMate, relationships. Few of them have a marriage that *I* would choose, however. Being SoulMates is an elevated quality of relationship, but the particular way that quality is experienced looks different for each couple. Characteristics that work very well for Jim and me may not work for you and your partner. Things that we dream of for our future together may not appeal to you at all. During a workshop a few months ago, a young husband said that one of the things he appreciated was that we only taught tools—each couple could build their own unique relationship using these tried and true tools.

Basically all homes are built with the same tools . . . hammers, saws, plumb lines, levels, and trowels to name just a few. Some use predominantly more stone, or steel or wood. Although the house built of stone has a very different look and feel than a house built of wood or steel, each of those is a material of integrity and strength—one is not necessarily better than the other, just different.

Drawing up plans for a house has some similarities to planning a wedding. As different factors are determined—the size, the materials, the layout of the floor plan and the style you prefer—the ideas can be translated into a blueprint that begins to pull the dream toward reality just as the initial vision described in a wedding planning journal becomes reality on the wedding day. The more specific the plans are, the more likely it is that the vision will becoming a reality.

Peter's simple dream of a puppy became over time more specifically a "big dog with many colors and spots." I believe that the more vividly he visualized his dog, a particular puppy we named "Lady" came closer to being a physical reality. The more clearly a dream is dreamed, the closer it is to fulfillment.

In one study five percent of the members of a Harvard graduating class had written their goals on paper. Through an alumni follow-up survey ten years later, researchers discovered that the same five percent who had written down their goals made ninety-five percent of the total income attributed to that particular class. Defining goals clearly enough to write them down is very powerful, indeed.

Jim loves golf. For Father's Day last year, his daughters gave him a philosophical novel that delivers its message via a golfing story.[9] A caddy named "Bagger Vance" appears just in time to help a has-been reclaim his skill in order to participate in a renowned tournament. Bagger Vance, in the movie by the same name, advises the pro to block out everything—every sand trap, every pond, every obstruction—and focus only on the field, "nothin' but the field." One of the points the story makes is to focus intensely, only at what you want, rather than what you want to avoid!

Sometime after my first husband died, I decided that I wanted to remarry. I made a list of the qualities I wanted in a husband. There were twenty or more items. One that I clearly remember was a sense of humor. There had been little humor in my life up until that time! I enjoyed sewing, so I made pink lace baby-doll pajamas as a "down payment" on the fulfillment of my dream, and hung them in a plastic bag in my closet. I was determined to wear them only for my (envisioned) husband.

Several years went by. I lost the list. Every time I cleaned out my closet I would come close to giving the p.j.s away. I lost confidence that this specific goal setting stuff would really work! But, you've read our story! The first several weeks we were dating I didn't think I was interested in Jim long term, but I kept saying "yes" to his date invitations because we had so much fun! A very special night eventually arrived when I wore my pink baby-doll pajamas for the man of my dreams, a man who has a wonderful sense of humor!

You may have identified a little (or a lot) of work that needs to be done in order to consistently experience a SoulMate relationship. A powerful way to speed up the journey—to bring the destination closer, faster, is to draw your own detailed blueprints for the way you want your marriage to eventually function—how you want it to look, to feel, to be—this shelter for your SoulMate love.   Doing the exercises suggested in "How to #1" as well as this book is a little like pushing your marriage down the highway—it will get you to your destination.   The more vivid your SoulMate relationship is in your

---

[9] Pressfield, Steven, (1995). <u>The Legend of Bagger Vance, a novel of golf and the game of life.</u>
New York: Avon Books.

imagination, however, the more that image will magnetically pull the marriage toward SoulMate status, meaning you won't have to push as hard.

The balance of this chapter is designed to help you create blueprints for your very own SoulMate relationship that will express in vivid detail exactly what you and your partner want to build together.

Every creation begins with an idea, an inspiration, a design. This is your chance to choose what, for you, would be an ideal marriage. Consider every aspect of your lives together. What initially attracted you to your spouse? How would those characteristics contribute to a SoulMate marriage? What attributes do you admire in him or her now? What would you like to be the dominant characteristics of your family life? What atmosphere do you desire in your home? How do you want to consistently treat each other? How would you ideally envision your finances, your vacations, your dates, your daily interactions, your decision making, your love making?

Use short, simple, first person, present tense statements, as though describing a relationship that already exists. Cover as many parts of your life together as you choose.

Example:

The atmosphere in our home is peaceful and loving.

We speak respectfully to one another.

If issues arise, we work out solutions respectfully.

A romantic air of being "in love" frequently sparkles between us.

Our love-making is passionate and mutually satisfying.

Warning: The first draft of almost every "blueprint" done by couples in my private practice is a description of how each partner wants the spouse to act or be. It isn't describing a marriage, but a marriage *partner.* You already have a partner, so adjust your wording to describe the *marriage*—the partnership.

This exercise may be done very effectively if only one partner participates. If you *are* doing this alone, complete your SoulMate

Blueprint as thoroughly as you can, describing your ideal of a SoulMate marriage. Make a special date with your partner to share it when he or she will not be distracted.

You might prepare him or her by saying something like, "I'm reading a book about how to improve a marriage. The book's author recommends creating a vivid picture of our relationship ideal. It's similar to the process of drawing detailed blueprints for a house so the builder knows exactly what is to be built. I really care about you and our relationship. Could I have some special time alone with you on Saturday? I'd like to share my ideas about what I hope our relationship can be. I want to hear about what is important to you, also. I want to include your desires in this blueprint." (Warning: If you are doing this exercise on your own, be especially careful to weed out statements that may be interpreted as manipulative messages to get your partner to change!)

If your spouse isn't willing to directly contribute, then create your SoulMate Blueprint anyway. As much as you can, include desires that your spouse has verbalized in the past. Your partner may have said, "Your work is more important to you than I am," or screamed during a fight, "Don't walk away when I'm talking to you!" Statements that would reflect healing of those issues might be:

Our relationship is our highest priority.

We respectfully listen to each other's feelings and points of view.

If an issue arises, we resolve it in a way that satisfies both of us.

It is even more powerful if both partners are willing to co-create the SoulMate Blueprint. If both are participating, each write out your individual blueprint of ideal characteristics. Make a date to share your first-person, present-tense statements. When you share, face each other, and as much as possible, look into your partner's eyes as you say your statements. Your deep desire for a great marriage with this person, and your willingness to be vulnerable are communicated by soft eye contact.

When you have shared, make a consolidated blueprint, combining your separate lists by eliminating duplicate or similar statements. Make a copy for each of you, and one to post on the refrigerator or bathroom mirror where you both will read it often.

The first time we did this exercise, we were amazed by two things—how hard it was to identify and write down exactly what we wanted (it was easier to say what we *didn't* want) and the similarity of our desires for our marriage. We were deeply touched by each other's vulnerability in revealing such precious dreams. We were in tears, as most couples are who complete this assignment. Just the acknowledgment of such deep longing for a good relationship is, in itself, healing.

We completed this exercise several years ago. For many months we read it together before going to sleep and it was taped to our refrigerator. Recently, we found the original exercise, and were elated to discover that 19 of the 20 statements are now consistently true in our relationship. Those were things like mutual respect, compassionate listening, clear communication, peaceful atmosphere, lots of laughter and thoughtfulness. One of the statements is still a work in process. Just like a house that periodically needs remodeling to suit new needs, or redecorating for up-to-date taste, we recently formulated a new, SoulMate Blueprint based on the next phase that we envision for our future together.

Remember "homeostasis" from Chapter Two of "How to Stay Married & Love It!"? We tend to resist change. You may find yourself resisting this exercise. It may seem hokey. Your relationship may be in such distress that you think this can't possibly help. You may want to concentrate on the really important stuff. We hope you take our word for it. This is really important!

So, get out your calendar. Make a date with yourself to work on and complete your SoulMate Blueprint. Talk to your spouse. Make a date to share. Mark a third date on your calendar when your revised or combined SoulMate Blueprint will be complete and copies of it placed where you see them often. Read it a minimum of once a day. For how long?   Until your experience—the reality of your SoulMate relationship—matches the statements on the paper!

Michele Weiner Davis[10] has some great suggestions for the process of making the dream a reality—breaking progress down into small, specific, bite-sized pieces. For instance, if your statement is "The atmosphere in our home is happy and peaceful," what could you do in the next two weeks that would move you toward that goal? Ask for a mirroring session when you feel irritated about something? Call a "time out" for yourself when you're about to use Defective Communication Tools?[11] Choose to mirror your spouse's feelings when he or she is upset rather than argue? Choose to give your spouse that special love-gift that you've resisted giving?[12] Small, separate, specific acts turn the vision represented by The Marriage Blueprint into reality. The power of the vision inspires and energizes those small, separate, specific acts.

The final step in this process is, perhaps, the most challenging. Without it this is just another "power of positive thinking" exercise. Don't get me wrong! There *is* power in the vision and positive thinking! But the reality is that positive thinking, alone, doesn't always give us the desired outcome. I believe that is because, ultimately, our vision of what is best for us is limited by our *wants*. The ultimate step is to then surrender the vision. One teacher I highly respect says to add "This or something better for the highest good of all concerned" to every vision. This statement, or one like it, ("I surrender to the Wisdom of the Universe," or "I trust what is best for me will manifest,") reflects some humility—I may not always see the big picture or understand what is best for everyone involved. If you're of the Christian persuasion, it would be appropriate to add, "Thy will be done." Many believe that four-word prayer is the most powerful prayer in all of scripture.

So, indeed, create your vision. Believe in it. Work toward it. And trust that the outcome will be what is in the best interests of everyone involved. There will be more about this concept in the final chapter of this volume entitled, "Ultimate SoulMates."

---

[10] Davis, Michele Weiner, (2001). <u>The Divorce Remedy</u>. New York: Simon & Schuster.
[11] Review Chapter 6, "Playing Detective," in <u>How to Stay Married & Love It!</u>
[12] See Chapters 3-5.

Puzzle Piece #6: Design the SoulMate Marriage of Your Dreams.

"I am courageously putting my vision of a SoulMate marriage on
paper and patiently bringing it into reality by each act of love,
while humbly surrendering the
ultimate outcome to Wisdom greater than myself."

"I like to think of the mind as a room.
In that room, we keep all of our usual ideas about life, God,
what's possible and what's not.
The room has a door. That door is ever so slightly ajar,
and outside we can see a great deal of dazzling light.
Out there in the dazzling light are a lot of new ideas
that we consider too far-out for us,
and so we keep them out there.
The ideas we are comfortable with are in the room with us.
The other ideas are out, and we keep them out. . .
More than anything else, recovery is an
exercise in open-mindedness.
Begin, this week, to consciously practice opening your mind."
Julia Cameron[13]

"Any enterprise is built by wise planning."
Proverbs 24:3

"What is faith?
It is the confident assurance that something we want
is going to happen.
It is the certainty that what we hope for is waiting for us,
even though we cannot see it up ahead."
Hebrews 11:1

Cameron, Julia, (1992). The Artist's Way, page 51. New York: G.P. Putnam's Sons
Publishers.

Puzzle Piece #7:

SoulMate Thoughtfulness

Chapter 3

Striking It Rich!

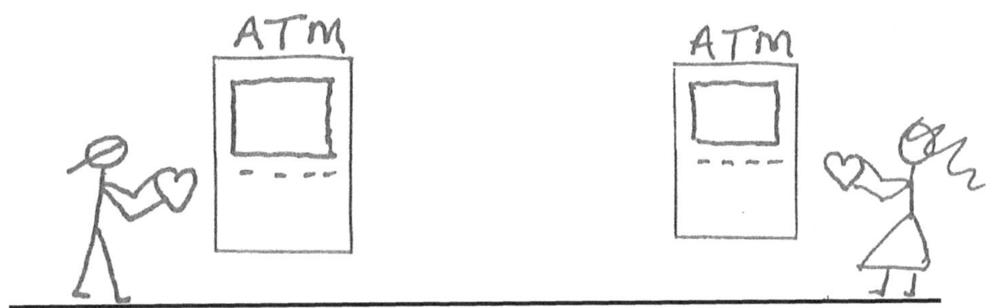

"The (first generation) millionaire population contains a disproportionately high concentration of people who tell me that integrity is a critical factor in explaining their success. . . (they) believe that *integrity begins at home.*"
(Italics mine)
Dr. Thomas Stanley[14]

Some time ago I cut an article out of our local paper entitled, "Couple in Costa Mesa marks 75th Anniversary!"[15]   The reporter asked, "What's your secret?"   While sitting in her rocking chair with John, 96, nodding off in his easy chair, Ellen said, "First of all, divorce was not an option. We just didn't believe in it." She said that they kept quarrels to a minimum and always respected each other. After thinking some more she added, "John always pulled into the driveway on time after work each evening." She went on to say that she always had dinner on the table and he always complimented her cooking. "He said I was the best!"

---

[14] Stanley, Dr. Thomas, (2000). <u>The Millionaire Mind</u>, pgs. 52, 60. Kansas City, MO: Andrews McMeel Publishing.
[15] Basheda, Lori, <u>The Orange County Register</u>, Morning, August 21, 1997.

The reporter asked them if they ever expected to be married this long, and Ellen pithily answered, "I didn't even expect to *live* this long!"

I have no idea what their financial picture was like, but they sounded as if they have enjoyed a rich life together.

Those of us who struggle to make our dollars cover our commitments are tempted to look with envy on those who have fat bank accounts. At the same time, most of us probably feel a little smug when we hear of a person who comes to the end of his or her life with a fortune in money but penniless when it comes to loving relationships. End-of-life stories like that of the millionaire, Howard Hughes, who died mentally ill, bereft of even one truly loving relationship, remind us that there is more to wealth than money.

Those who have major health challenges, often name good health as the primary condition of a wealthy life; yet, Christopher Reeve[16] and other disabled persons of such clarity of spirit prove that a life wealthy in purpose and love can be successfully lived in spite of enormous physical limitations.

There are ways of living that result in destitution even if the bank balance is fat, and there are ways of living that result in wealth no matter how skinny the purse.

One of the ways to be wealthy is to enjoy a great marriage relationship. If the term "SoulMates" is what attracted you to our books, having a great marriage must be a high priority for you. You, like us, may have experienced a heart-tug while reading of John and Ellen. Perhaps, like us, you thought, "I want a marriage like that," or, "I hope we have that much time to enjoy each other," or, "Someday I hope we'll be interviewed to share our great marriage secrets." Others of you may have thought, "I'd give everything I own to have a marriage like that," or, "We have more work to do, but that is the kind of relationship we are building."

The concept of a Marriage Bank Account[17] helps us to apply the concrete process of wealth building to the inexact science of building

---

[16] Reeve, Christopher, (1998). <u>Still Me</u>, New York: Random House Publishers.
[17] Harley, Willard F. Jr., (1992). <u>Love Busters</u>, Grand Rapids, Michigan: Flemming H. Revell Publishers.

a wealthy marriage. It is a simple way of quantifying the various things we each do that impact the other, either positively or negatively in order to communicate more clearly. The following "check registers" demonstrate how this works. (In bookkeeping language, numbers in parentheses are minus in value, or withdrawals. We made the values 1 through 10 so that the scale is the same as the one we recommend you use in Book #1, Chapter 9 when you practice mirroring.)

Jim's Account:	Value:	Nancy's Account	Value:
Things Nancy did:		Things Jim did:	
Greeted me at the door	$ 4	Gave flowers for anniversary	$10
Surprise gift of golf clubs	$10	Vacuumed the house	$ 5
Fetched something for me	$ 2	Put laundered clothes away	$ 5
Played table games to please me	$ 4	Promised night out but forgot	($4)
Was crabby with me	($2)	I dented fender, kind, no lecture	$ 8
Cleaned up kitchen without me	$ 3	Made big decision without me	($6)
Teased me about sensitive issue	($5)	Told me I'm a classy lady!	$ 8
Respects way I handled an issue	$10	Ran to the market for me	$ 2
Initiated lovemaking	$10	Cuddled me while we talked	$10

Before I take this any further, please don't misunderstand the purpose of this metaphor. Jim and I have never "kept a running tally" as shown in this illustration, and are not suggesting that you "keep score" either! In our efforts to communicate more clearly, however, giving a numerical value to "deposits" and "withdrawals" helps us understand how appreciated or how hurtful various acts are.

Some withdrawals are minor annoyances. Others, such as physical abuse or infidelity can bankrupt a marriage. Some deposits are small favors. Other deposits are definitely 10s! The determination of the value is an individual thing and may vary from day to day, depending on the circumstances. Sometimes Jim is surprised when he does something for me that, to him, is worth perhaps $1 or $2 but to me is worth $10! A withdrawal that to me seems only a minus $1 may feel to *him* like a minus $6. I may do something for Jim intending it to be a deposit, but to him it's a withdrawal! Discovering the differences in the value we each assign to a specific withdrawal or deposit gives us valuable information about each other.

Jim: "Some of us guys like to make occasional big deposits—the "grand gesture"—but we may neglect the little daily deposits that add up to a great marriage. Taking my wife out to a nice restaurant for dinner and then to a hit stage play once a month, does not make up for coming home an hour late three times last week, and leaving my dirty socks on the bedroom floor every night!

Here's an illustration we understand: if a young couple 25 years of age begin depositing $25 per month into a retirement account, and continue to do that for the next 40 years, their deposits plus the accrued interest at a conservative 8 percent will total well over $1,000,000 by the time they retire! Small, regular deposits add up to a wealthy bank account—and a wealthy marriage!

"When I give Nancy a compliment such as 'You look beautiful. I like that dress' I think it's only worth $1—it didn't cost me anything, it's true, and it's easy to say; but Nancy tells me a compliment is worth a minimum of $5 to her and might be worth $10, depending on how badly she needs to hear it.

"On the other hand, when I bring home a bouquet of flowers for her, I think it's worth $10 every time—it cost me money and in three or four days it's dead and must be thrown away. To Nancy, the value varies depending on how she's feeling—never less than a $6 but some days a $10.

"On the withdrawal side of the ledger, if I commit both of us to attend a meeting without conferring with Nancy, I may think it should only be a $1 withdrawal, but to her it's a minus $5.

"This concept has really helped me learn about Nancy. After all, she's the one I intend to be with for the rest of my life. If I can avoid large withdrawals, and learn to make consistent deposits to her account, my life is going to be a lot more enjoyable. Also, when I mess up, I want lots of money in her account so she'll go easy on me. Both of us have found that forgiveness for minor withdrawals comes more quickly when our bank account is full. It's harder to be forgiving if the bank account is flirting with non-sufficient-funds status!"

Sometimes our attempts to be helpful turn out to be more frustrating to our partner than helpful! One of the most valuable questions Jim ever asks is "What can I do to help?" He's learned to make the most of his desire to build up my bank account by making sure that his actions count as a deposit rather than a withdrawal!

Here's some other ideas:

Would it help you if I...took the kids to the park for a while to give you a break?

How about if I...order Chinese home delivery for dinner tonight?

Until this big project is complete, what would give you the most relief...fixing a sack lunch so you can work through your lunch hour? Or getting the neighbor to mow the lawn so that is off of your list? Or both!

You get the picture. They are simple questions that give you pointers about how to best make a positive difference in your partner's life *today*. What counts is that you genuinely want to help relieve pressure, or reduce a temporary over-load of responsibilities or provide emotional support and encouragement.

It's essential to only offer things that you can give or do without resentment. Resentment *kills* relationship! And it's important to remember the kindnesses that your partner has done for you! At times, life seems to provide a natural ebb and flow to the need for giving and receiving of help. Some days/weeks we're on the giving end—other times we're the receiver.

Which leads to another truth about this concept: Although there will be times when one of you needs more thoughtfulness than the other, it's ultimately death to a SoulMate relationship if one person is *always* the giver and the other *always* the receiver. In a

SoulMate marriage, both partners make it a high priority to keep a high balance of thoughtfulness in each other's bank accounts!

Puzzle Piece #7: Build a SoulMate marriage one thoughtful deposit at a time.

"I will ask and look for a minimum of three thoughtful things to do or say *each day* to build up my partner's bank account."

"A wealthy marriage is the result of a lifetime of large and small acts of love and thoughtfulness by both partners."
Jim and Nancy Landrum

"A wise person builds his (her) house while a foolish person tears his (hers) down by his (her) own efforts."
Proverbs 14:1

Chapter 4

Do You Speak the Language?

**Harry fell asleep watching Monday Night football
and spent the night on the couch.
The next morning, his wife woke him and said,
"Get up, dear. It's 20 to 7."
Harry opened his eyes and asked, "In whose favor?"
Anonymous**

About two months ago our bank decided they needed all of their customers to change the routing number for on-line banking. They sent detailed instructions for the "simple" procedure. After several days of mentally fortifying myself, I woke up one morning and told myself, "This is the day." I sat down at the computer and very, very carefully began following their instructions. My banking program, of course, would not allow me do those "simple" maneuvers. One of those aggravating windows kept popping up meaning that I'd hit a dead-end.

I resigned myself to calling the 24-hour help line. There was just one problem. A big one. Because I haven't learned computer language, I knew I would fumble around trying to describe what was happening. When the helper finally understood what I meant, he would give me directions that I wouldn't understand. He would, with professional patience, try to reduce the solution to baby steps in regular English so (I hoped) I could do what he was suggesting.

That day I spent three hours both on the bank's help line and the computer program manufacturer's help line. Neither of them could figure out what was wrong. Finally I was referred to a technical assistant whose office in the East had closed for the day. The next morning I called *that* number. With this call, I graduated from 800 numbers to a toll line. Now the phone company was billing me for the call, plus I got to pay by the minute for the technical assistant.

After about 30 minutes, the next guy up the helper chain was *sure* he had solved the problem for me. He sounded self-satisfied and elated. I *hoped* he had solved it. After hanging up, I completed the rest of the procedure. The new routing number successfully worked, but according to my record, I also had about $35,000 more in our checking account than either the bank or I thought I had! His *solution* had wiped out multiple transactions over the three years I had used this program. Other transactions had parts missing. It took me several hours to repair all of this year's transactions. The rest I "fixed" with a balance adjustment after the most recent bank statements arrived. If they ever need to change routing numbers again, I will change banks!

To add insult to injury, each of the "helpers" started out with a condescending tone of voice, because they assumed the problem was with my incompetence. They made that assumption because I didn't speak intelligent computer-ese! At first I made the same assumption. As it turned out, the problem was a mysterious glitch in the program, not my incompetence. My inability to speak their language, however, complicated the process.

A very dear husband and wife come to our home every two weeks to give it a thorough cleaning. They are sweet, trustworthy, and do a better job than I would. Any major change in our routine, however, requires the intervention of their young daughter who speaks both their language and mine. Any but the most elementary communications are complicated because we don't share a common language.

Besides the thousands of ethnic languages in the world, there are special languages that go with every industry and profession. When Steven got his private pilot's license, he had to learn the language that would enable him to be understood by air traffic controllers all over the country. When Peter became a highway patrolman, he learned the special codes and language shortcuts of that service. His wife, Shelley, a nurse, shares a medical language with other emergency room personnel. For many years, our son-in-law, Greg, worked as a stunt man, and our daughter, Teri, worked as an actress in Hollywood. The movie industry has its own language for every piece of equipment and every kind of "shot." Karen's bookkeeping job and her husband, Matt's, plumbing job both come with their own languages. For successful communication, it is a severe disadvantage not to know the ethnic or professional language of the one to whom you are speaking.

Love also has its languages. The language that communicates love the most effectively to me may not be the same that communicates love to you.

Gary Chapman has written a great book about the different languages that express love.[18] What follows is a brief synopsis of the five love languages he has identified. All of us have one *primary* language, although we may enjoy all five ways of receiving love.

WORDS OF AFFIRMATION

Jim: "Although I gladly receive Nancy's expressions of love no matter how they are delivered, I especially appreciate her *words* of affirmation that let me know I have her respect. I *want* her love, but need her *respect* even more. During our tough years, she finally told me that she loved me no matter what, but respect was something that had to be earned. Earning her respect became one of my most powerful motivations for doing the difficult work needed in order to save our marriage. Even today, I never feel more loved and valued than when she *tells* me how much she respects me.

"The power of what we communicate with words is awesome. Because my mother often gave me words of encouragement— telling me I could do anything I wanted to do—I never

---

[18] Chapman, Gary. (December, 1992). <u>The Five Love Languages</u>. Chicago: Moody Press.

questioned my ability to be successful. Her encouraging words also told me how much she loved me.

"Both Nancy and I love to hear the words 'I love you' and we say them to each other often."

Other ways that communicate love with words are pet names and notes. I love for Jim to call me his "sugar baby." He loves to be my "handsome devil." I treasure every handwritten note that Jim has ever given me . . . I have a huge file folder stuffed with them. On my desk at this moment is a card with a hand written note expressing his pride in me for sending the book proposal for this manuscript to some literary agents in New York. He adds, "I love you and I love watching you bloom! Thank you for saying 'yes' almost 20 years ago. I'm so glad you did! All my love, Jim." You can be sure that this card will be in my possession until the day I die!

I *thought* I had completed this chapter when Jim and I decided to quiz each other about the things that make us feel the most loved today. (We hadn't done this for about five years.) We found that the expressions of love that were once new and reassuring, are now so integrated into our relationship that we take them for granted. They are still *very* appreciated, but as our relationship is evolving there are new words that don't so much say "I love you," but that make us *feel* loved, nevertheless.

Jim: "Every time Nancy says 'Yeah, Jim!' when I am riding my exercise bicycle, (something I don't like doing) I know she wants me to live a long time and I feel loved. Every time she encourages me to play golf, especially when it isn't my usual golfing day, I feel loved."

I, too, know I am loved when Jim encourages me to get a massage. I felt *incredibly* loved when he told me that he wanted me to go back to school for my master's degree. I *knew* I was loved when he agreed to the loans to pay for it. I feel *so* loved when he tells me he believes in my ability to write. He tells me I am a gifted counselor, and whether I am or not, I feel loved.

Words of love are precious, whether they specifically say, "I love you," or the fact is implied by other words of caring and encouragement. The next chapter, "A World- Wide Famine," expands on the theme of important words we can say to others, but especially our spouse. For many, words are the primary vehicle that communicates love.

GIFTS

One of my clients feels the *most* loved when her husband picks up little gifts and brings them home to her. The expense of the gift isn't what is important to her. It can be a package of her favorite chewing gum! She says what makes her feel so loved is that he was thinking of her while they were apart and took the time and effort to find something that he knew would please her.

Jim and I sometimes plan mystery dates for each other. We agree that what we actually *do* on those dates is secondary. Love is communicated by the *gift* of effort that has gone into the planning of the date.

In the giving of gifts, it's important to find out how your partner likes to receive gifts. Does your partner appreciate being asked what he or she wants so the gift is not a surprise, but sure to please? Does your partner want to be surprised, but appreciates the gift being one from a suggested list? Does your partner feel loved when little nonsense gifts are tucked in his socks or does she like to find a chocolate kiss in her lingerie drawer?

Jim loves getting things he *needs* for his birthday or Christmas. He appreciates it when I notice that his handkerchiefs or socks are getting shabby and wrap up new ones for his birthday. He loves getting books of crossword puzzles. (He's an addict. He has them stashed in his nightstand, his briefcase and his car!) He loves little gadgets that meet some practical need.

I love getting gift certificates so I have the thoughtfulness of the gift, but get to choose something I particularly like. In fact, when Jim asks, I tell him two or three things I would like that he can choose from, and then add that I'd like one little surprise. I feel loved just knowing that Jim keeps a file in his briefcase where he tucks notes about someplace I might like to visit or things that he may give to me.

This Christmas we got a gift certificate from one of our children to a favorite restaurant and gift certificates for movies from another. We'd much rather get something that we need or would be sure to use than a very beautiful, expensive item that sits on a shelf. But that's us. It may not be your or your SoulMate's preference. Find out how to give gifts that effectively communicate your love!

ACTS OF SERVICE

Because I have had injuries to my back, I have to be careful when I do certain activities, or I will need several visits to the chiropractor. One of the jobs that is the hardest on my back is vacuuming. Several years ago, Jim volunteered to take over the vacuuming chore. Every time I hear Jim running the vacuum, I know I am loved.

Jim: "Nancy does all of the meal preparation at our house. Because she does the cooking, I usually clean up the dishes now that there are no longer children at home to help with that job. When I've had an especially long day, and Nancy knows I'm tired, she will shoo me out of the kitchen after dinner, doing the clean-up herself. Her kind consideration for me makes me feel very loved.

"I feel loved when she shops for clothes for me to give to my mother . . . and then alters them to fit her. I feel *very* loved when she makes all of the arrangements for our vacations, and pays our bills, and prepares for the tax appointment or bakes cornbread for me.

"Some acts of love are more subtle. Because we are a step-family, I feel loved because Nancy loves my children and has worked hard to build good relationships with them. The grandchildren are *our* grandchildren, something we both appreciate in each other."

Neither of us holds a nine-to-five job. Between the two of us, Jim frequently has the most demanding schedule. Because my schedule is usually more flexible, I am the one to buy groceries, shop for office supplies, dog food, and gifts, do our bills and bookkeeping and go to the post office or bank. I began writing this book in earnest, however, during the time of year when Jim is the least busy, so he made me this offer, "Anything that needs doing, tell me about it first. If I can, I'll do it. I want to support you by taking over any of the chores that I can." After just a few days, I told him I could get used to this! I feel *very* loved because of his *acts* of service.

QUALITY TIME SPENT TOGETHER

After carefully evaluating my feelings when Jim has said "I love you" in each of the five love languages, I realized I feel the *most* loved when he gives me his undivided attention. I've mentioned in Book #1 that I can count on him to listen to me when I need to talk. Also, part of the *gift* of a mystery date is that he intends to spend *quality time* with me. From the first days of our marriage, he's insisted that we spend some time every week doing something we enjoy together. One of the things that appealed to me the most about Jim was his ability to set aside quality time for fun.

The times our family gets together are quality times, because we listen to each other and have fun. Because we all have so much to say to each other, we've developed a system . . . if you want to talk, you raise your finger signaling that when the current story teller is finished, it will be your turn next! Jim has spent a lot of quality time listening to my sons. Quality time, in a marriage, a family, or a friendship communicates love. Quality times occasionally happen spontaneously, but in today's frenetic culture must usually be planned.

Years ago I read a little booklet called "Tyranny of the Urgent."[19] It was about our tendency to let petty but demanding little tasks eat up our time so there is nothing left for truly important things. Stephen Covey[20] suggest putting the tasks of highest priority on the calendar first, then the next important, down to the least important. Other systems have us label tasks A, B, or C, depending on their importance. That way quality time is allotted for a date with your spouse every week, your son's ballgame, or shopping with your daughter for a prom dress *before* you schedule a nail appointment, cleaning the kitchen, mowing the lawn, or a business dinner. These tools help insure that our time is spent in alignment with our true priorities. How we spend our time *does* demonstrate the priority of our relationships.

---

[19] Hummel, Charles E., "Tyranny of the Urgent." 1977, IL: InterVarsity Press.
[20] Covey, S. 1989. <u>Seven Habits of Highly Effective People</u>. New York: Simon & Schuster, Fireside.

Quality time tip: Quality time includes setting aside time to speak, listen and work out solutions to issues. The annoying or hurtful issues that arise in any relationship will only grow larger and more destructive with neglect. Quality time also includes time for relaxation, fun, catching up, romance—and all the other essential ingredients to a SoulMate marriage. But—and listen! This is important!—don't mix the two! It's *either* a date to work out an issue *or* a date to enjoy each other. If an "issue" comes up during a time planned for fun, set a time to deal with it later and resume your fun. And, be sure to keep the date to deal with the issue! Both types of quality time are necessary for a SoulMate marriage, but need to be kept separate!

AFFECTIONATE TOUCH

After being single for 13 years, I was loving-touch deprived. We've been married almost 22 years and Jim is still making up for those years that were barren of romantic touch. (He's not complaining!) Loving touch is definitely an important part of a SoulMate relationship. For some, however, it is the *primary* way that they receive the knowledge that they are loved. Sexual intimacy is included in this category, of course, but it is more than that. It is hugs while passing in the hallway, a gentle swat on the behind, holding hands, sitting arm in arm, or cuddling at the end of the day. Sometimes Jim puts his warm hand on the back of my neck when we're walking someplace. Sometimes I come up behind him while he's working at the table and kiss his ear. Every gentle or playful touch communicates love.

Loving touch is essential not just for lovers, but for the health of every human being. Gentle, loving touches actually create chemical changes in our bodies that facilitate a healthier immune system. Those who live alone are healthier even when they only have an animal with whom to be affectionate.

When my boys became old enough to be self-conscious about being hugged and kissed in front of their friends, I would wait until I was home alone with one of them. I'd say, "Come here and let me hold you. Nobody is home. No one will know. I promise I won't tell." They'd sheepishly come to me, sit on my knee or beside me and let me hug and kiss them for a few minutes, while telling them how much I loved them.

My mother had a collection of beautiful glass pieces. One of them was a serving bowl made out of "carnival" glass that arrived in a large sack of flour when my grandmother was a new bride. She also had several pieces of "depression" glass and "milk" glass.

Several years ago while meandering through an antique store, I spotted a beautiful little cream pitcher made out of cranberry colored glass. I am not a connoisseur of glass, but I thought this little pitcher was charming. Mom's birthday was coming up and the pitcher fit my budget, so I bought it for her. This thought went through my mind as I was paying for it, "Maybe someday Mom will tire of it or won't want it anymore, then I might get this back!"

Recently Mom moved from a large home to a small apartment in a senior living center. She moved only the absolute necessities and her most treasured items. She invited all her kids and grandkids to her house to take whatever we wanted before someone came to haul the rest away. You guessed it—I got the cranberry glass pitcher!

Have *you* ever purchased a gift for someone because *you* liked it? Have you ever received a gift that was a perfect example of the *giver's* style but wasn't "you" at all? It's a fairly common frailty of humans to give the gift we wish we were getting!

When it comes to expressing love, we often make the same mistake. We *give* love in the way we most like to *get* love. The problem is that the way you give it may not be the most effective way to communicate "I love you" to the receiver, so the full benefit of the message is lost. You may not be speaking his or her love language.

We recommend that you make a date with your spouse for the express purpose of exploring each other's love languages. Ask questions like, "What 10 things have I done in the past that have made you feel the most loved?" Write down all the answers. See if a majority of them fall into one of the five categories. Ask your spouse to rate the love languages from first to last in importance.

Of the couples we know who have done this, there has occasionally been a husband and wife who share the same primary love language. They are lucky. Many of the rest of us, though, may be giving love in the way we wish to receive it, rather than the way that means the most to our spouse. When that is true, it becomes a sacrifice of love to train oneself to give love to the spouse via the language of the spouse's preference.

My parents communicated their love in other languages, but didn't use words of affirmation. Consequently, I wasn't comfortable verbalizing words of praise or encouragement. That love language wasn't my "native" language. So when I learned that "words of affirmation" was Jim's primary love language—that he actually hungered for words that acknowledged his value—that *words* were what made him feel the most loved—I had a major learning curve ahead of me! I had to consciously remind myself to *verbalize* my feelings of appreciation or admiration for Jim. In the beginning it was even hard to think of how to put the sentences together! But over time, words of affirmation became a comfortable and valuable new habit that spilled over into my relationships with my children and friends. I am a better wife, mother and friend—a better human being—because I made the effort to learn how to deliver my love to Jim in a language he needed to hear!

Besides being a service, lavishly loving one's spouse in the language of the spouse's choice is a healthy kind of selfish thing to do. When your partner's love bank account is full because he/she has received love in the language of their choice, they will have abundant resources from which to love you back! When Jim and I began dating, I was very cautious. I'd been very hurt in a previous relationship. Jim sensed my fear and finally told me, "Your loving cup has been drained dry. I'm going to love you, and love you, and love you, until your cup overflows and you love me back!" That's exactly what he proceeded to do! It worked!

It's rare to find someone so damaged that they can consistently resist the most powerful force in the world—love. It is nearly impossible to pour yourself into the service of generously giving love to your spouse without the love eventually being given back to you in the same measure. Learning to speak his or her language is a thoughtful *and* smart act of loving service that SoulMates gladly do for each other.

Puzzle Piece #6: SoulMates learn to speak love in each other's language.

"I will consciously choose to *frequently* deliver love
in the preferred language of my partner."

**"I don't know what your destiny will be, but one thing I do know: the only ones among you who will be really happy are those who have sought and found how to serve."
Albert Schweitzer[21]**

"*It is possible to give away and become richer!
It is also possible to hold on too tightly and lose everything.
Yes, the liberal man shall be rich!
By watering others, he waters himself.*"
Proverbs 11:24,25

---

[21] Schweitzer, Albert, from a sermon entitled, "The Life of Service" delivered to the Church of St. Nicolai in Strasbourg sometime between 1900 to 1919. Published in 1947 in the first English version of The Philosophy of Civilization and The Ethics of Reverence of Life, Chapter 26. Beacon Press.

Chapter 5

A World-Wide Famine

**". . . abundance and lack are parallel realities;
every day I make the choice of which
one to inhabit."
Sarah Ban Breathnach**[22]

We don't like to think about the reality of famine. It's one of those unspeakable disasters that happen to other people, not us or those we love; yet we've all seen the photos. It is inconceivable that we could share a world that we know as so abundant with so many who are starving. While watching the appeals for donations on television programs, we feel appalled and helpless. Some give nothing because the little that can be given appears ludicrous in the face of so much need. Others give what they can even though they may never have the satisfaction of seeing with their own eyes the difference they've made.

Famine on the physical level is caused by inadequate nourishment to sustain health or life. There are other ways to starve, however. There is famine on the mental level—a lack of education. Some never have the opportunity to explore the world of knowledge, ideas, and theories. Others have the opportunity, but consume mental "food" at only a subsistence level, barely enough to survive in an increasingly complex world.

---

[22] Ban Breathnach, Sarah, (1995). Simple Abundance, a Daybook of Comfort and Joy, forward. New York: Warner Books.

Spiritual famine also exists—the hunger for meaning and purpose in life, the desire to deeply *know* that there is order and intelligence beyond our own.

The famine addressed in this chapter is a condition that every one of us has the power to alleviate. The craving I'm writing about cannot be satisfied with a Big Mac, a textbook or faith. It is the hunger to know that someone is *grateful* we are alive and the hunger of character that can only be filled by having a *grateful heart*. It is often buried, but we all hunger to have our accomplishments or our being *recognized*, to be *appreciated* for our efforts or character, and to be *encouraged* to own the magnificence of who we are or can be.

GRATITUDE

Our first grandson, Joey, was born on December 28th. A few days later on New Year's Day, when Teri and baby were safely home, the family gathered to celebrate his birth. I treasure a photograph taken of Joey lying on my chest as I was leaning back against the sofa pillows. We were both asleep. I remember our gratitude for his precious life.

We celebrated the early arrival of Jason, who was so tiny that only Karen, his Aunt Teri, and his grandmothers were brave enough to hold him. I had the honor of holding Alyssa just a few minutes after her birth and was privileged to be in the delivery room with Christian, the first to hold him, welcoming him into the world. Other than Pete and Shelley, I was the first family member to hold Katie. Two and one-half years later, I remember the late night call when Peter said, "Mom, I'm holding a little boy in my arms!" sharing with us the safe arrival of Nicholas.

Each of these children has been welcomed with gratitude into the loving arms of this family. Our hearts are *filled* with gratefulness for the unique individuals they are.

When my father was dying, my mother repeatedly told my sisters and me how grateful she was for our help. In her eighties, in spite of the difficulties of diabetes and arthritis, she continued to be a grateful person. She was grateful when I dropped by to see her, grateful to be driven to church, grateful for the nurse who dispensed her medication and the other employees who made her senior living complex such a pleasant, friendly place to live.

Having someone be grateful for my existence or my actions is a form of food that feeds my heart. This is nourishment that every one of us is capable of giving to another. There are dozens of times every day when it would be appropriate to say "Thank you" or "I'm grateful for you."

You may be diligent about saying "Thank you" to your secretary, your sales manager or the box boy at the grocery store. Wonderful, but when's the last time you told your wife or husband that you are grateful they said "yes"? How long has it been since you told your child that you are so grateful that he or she was delivered to you?   Is your gratitude for something they've *done* that pleases you or just because they are a treasured part of your life?

Gratitude is a precious gift to loved ones and strangers alike; but the benefit of *being* grateful goes even deeper. *Being* grateful changes a person's life. The author of <u>Simple Abundance</u>[23] said that we cannot list five things for which we are grateful every night for four months without our lives being changed. Six years ago I took the challenge. We were still struggling to recover from the financial reversals mentioned in Book #1. Every time I prepared a deposit, I thought, "This isn't going to be enough. I'm not sure how we're going to pay this bill." I fretted as though fretting would help. It didn't. I constantly felt squeezed by anxiety and was more aware of what we lacked than what we had.

I began keeping a "gratitude journal" as suggested. Every night I wrote down five things for which I was grateful that day. Sometimes I had to stretch to think of five, one of which was usually that I could finally go to bed! Gradually I began to express gratitude for every bill we successfully paid. The practice grew until I began consciously verbalizing gratitude for every dollar we deposited into our account. I would look out the kitchen window and say "thank you" to the grass for being so green. I expressed gratitude to Jim for his presence in my life, and his sweet kisses!

In October of that year I paid $1.79 for a package of seeds and a few months later had my breath stolen away by the wonder of 30 feet of fence covered by sweet pea vines more than 7 feet tall! As

---

[23] Breathnach, Sarah. (1995). <u>Simple Abundance: A Daybook of Comfort and Joy</u>. New York: Warner Books

Jim joined me in the practice of gratitude, we agreed the lavish flowers provided a living, full color demonstration of abundance! Although our financial condition had not significantly changed, I realized one day that I was *feeling rich.* The practice of gratitude changed my awareness from lack to wealth. Soon, we were amazed to see our income beginning to climb. Every financial responsibility was met on time. It is my belief that gratitude opened up a space inside us for more to be given. Worry and our focus on lack closed us down so there was no room for the blessings of more.

Jim feels loved when I express my gratitude for him in my life. He never gets tired of hearing me say how thankful I am for the work he did that helped us save our marriage. I never tire of hearing "Thank you for walking the dog," or "I'm grateful you're mine." Gratitude nourishes the soil in which love grows.

RECOGNITION

Some time ago I had the flu. I was miserable. I climbed into bed and turned on the television even though it usually bores me. I thought it would help me go to sleep quickly. Instead, I happened on the televising of Disney's Teacher of the Year awards. Hundreds of teachers had been considered and 30 of them were present in Boston for the finals. Film clips were shown of each teacher in action with quotes from his or her colleagues and students. It was incredibly inspiring! In spite of having to fight to keep my eyelids open, I couldn't turn it off!

There was one sad aspect of the ceremony, however. Of the ten who were called forward to receive this honor, almost every one of them, in tears, said something like, "This (recognition) never happens to us! We don't teach to get recognition, but this is just too wonderful!" How sad that people who wield so much influence over our children are starving for recognition!

It's sad when those who serve us are ignored, but it's tragic when those we *love* are starving for our recognition! If I'm not careful, my daily routine can blur my awareness that Jim comes home faithfully to me every night or that our grandchildren have loving, involved parents. It's not that I need to make a meaningless mantra of recognizing every little thing—recognition might even lose it's meaning if it were constant—but everyone deserves heart-felt recognition for the contributions that bless my life or bless those I love.

For my parents 50th wedding anniversary celebration, my sisters and I sent invitations to all the friends, former employees, family members, and church associates whom we could locate. We asked them, whether or not they could attend, to write letters describing a favorite memory of my folks or recognition for a kindness given, etc. They were mailed to me one week ahead of the party so I had time to fill a huge photo album with them. My mother had taken thousands of photos through the years, so we also prepared a slide show of the highlights of their lives, recognizing many of the qualities for which they were esteemed. My parents ate it up! Who wouldn't! The next day I found out that my dad was so jazzed that he sat up all night reading and rereading the letters from his children, grandchildren, friends and associates.

Why do we wait to give a gift that is so precious? It shouldn't require a 50th anniversary, retirement party, or even worse, a memorial service to recognize the gift of someone's life.

APPRECIATION

Recently we drove to San Diego to see Joey play in a baseball travel league. He is 16 years old, six-foot-four, and a terrific pitcher. He usually plays on weekends when we're unable to attend, so we were thrilled to get to see him play this Friday. His team had already won the first three elimination games and was expected to win this semi-final and go on to play the championship in the San Diego College Stadium.

One of Joey's teammates, however, had trouble controlling his mouth. Early in the game the umpire warned him to refrain from using certain words. In about the fifth inning, when they were ahead 10-9, the boy didn't like a call and let loose with the forbidden words. The umpire simply pointed his finger in the direction of the parking lot and said, loudly and clearly, "Out!" The boy was a star player and a team sparkplug at bat. According to the rules, being kicked out of one game meant he couldn't play in the next game, as well. He took it badly. It required several minutes and a lot of help for him to leave the premises. Joey's entire team was rattled, lost their lead, and then lost the game.

Afterwards, as he gathered his gear and was walking off the field, Jim approached the umpire and said, "I want to tell you how much I appreciate the good job of umpiring you did, and I especially appreciate your stand against profanity with these boys." The umpire's face broke into a gigantic grin as he replied, "Sir, you've made my day!" Jim went on to explain that the kid he booted was on *our* team. The ump said, "Now you've *really* made my day!"

Of the hundred or so adults there, Jim was the only one who expressed any appreciation to this underpaid, unassuming hero who had demonstrated his love for the boys during the game by frequent gentle pats and words of praise. I suppose he umpires many games in between the occasional words of appreciation from a coach, parent or kid.

One of my clients had complained several times about her husband's lack of appreciation for her. I suggested that she ask for it. She was shocked. Would it be right to ask for appreciation for things that are just her assigned jobs in the family? Yes! And it is also appropriate to frequently express appreciation to him for bringing home his paycheck, and any other of his tasks or traits that contribute to the successful running of the family and her quality of life!

Most of us are starving for appreciation. Just because I do the laundry every Monday doesn't mean I shouldn't be appreciated for it! I used to fold and hang and put away all of Jim's clean clothes. He assumed clean clothes would always be in the drawer or closet. Then I began leaving the folded items on the bed and the shirts hanging on the door jam. He put them away without comment the first week. The second week he asked why I was leaving them out. I answered, "Because I want to be appreciated for doing a job that I don't particularly enjoy." Now, as he's putting away his clean clothes, he rarely fails to tell me how much he appreciates them and me! His appreciation for me, and mine for him, feeds our desire to do more for each other—it keeps our respective bank accounts brimming over!

I've heard many people say that the only time they were noticed was when they had done something "bad." Why do we think it's O.K. to take for granted desirable behavior as though it's our right to get it from someone we love, and yet gripe or punish when that loved one does something that inconveniences us or of which we don't approve? It's long been a reported by psychologists, who have examined the matter, that we get more of whatever we reinforce with our attention. Negative attention for negative behavior generates more of the same. Positive attention for positive behavior generates more of the same. We choose what we want more of!

ENCOURAGEMENT

The last nourishing gift I'm going to discuss is encouragement. As he was growing up, Jim's mother repeatedly told him that he could do anything he wanted to do in life. He so thoroughly believed her that, even though he was socially awkward and insecure, it never occurred to him that he couldn't do whatever he chose as a profession. He consistently got top grades. From the age of eight he mowed lawns and by 14 years old was working the equivalent of three paper routes. As soon as he was old enough, he worked in a grocery store. He saved most of the money from all of these jobs for college. In spite of marrying after his first year of college, he supported his wife and first daughter while finishing college and graduate school. His beautiful baritone voice and youth choirs have been heard in hundreds of churches throughout the Southwest. At one time, in one church, he had more than 600 persons from toddlers to seniors involved in choirs. He's sold thousands of gospel music albums. He's sung the national anthem for the Los Angeles Lakers and Dodgers and dozens of Anaheim Angels ball games. He's done exactly what he wanted with his life, because his mother was willing to give him the encouragement he needed in order to thrive.

Florence Littauer, a highly respected speaker and author of numerous books, has delivered her "Silver Boxes" speech[24] to hundreds of audiences. In it, she likens giving precious words of encouragement to handing out little silver boxes with ribbons on them.

In that speech she tells about her father who ran a struggling corner grocery store during the years Florence and her brothers were growing up. Florence excelled in English and Composition, earning a scholarship to college. One day when she came home for the

---

[24] Her inspiring presentation is available as a book, cassette, or video from CLASServices, Inc. Phone #505-899-4283 or www.classervices.com.

weekend, her father took a small brown box out of hiding behind the piano. He opened it, showing her numerous articles he had written that had been published by community and denominational church papers. She had no idea he could write! She asked why he hadn't pursued writing as a profession. He shrugged his shoulders as he explained that her mother was afraid they would be embarrassed by rejection since he was "uneducated." Even though he had nurtured a broad and varied interest in literature and poetry in his children and had many letters to the editor published, he believed his wife. A few days later, he unexpectedly died, never having known the pleasure of doing what he loved for a living. His dream was never realized, in part because he was starved to death from lack of encouragement.

I've wanted to write a book since I learned to read. It was a secret desire, not one I dared to share with anyone. While a junior in high school, my English teacher gave us the assignment of reading a classic from the list he provided. We were to write and orally present a book report. I loved my choice and enjoyed writing about it. I was so timid I rarely spoke up in class, but for some reason he called on me to deliver the first book report. When I finished, my teacher immediately jumped up and said, "Now, *that* was a professional-quality book review!" Those eight words fanned the flame of my dream, and helped to keep it alive until I had time to do all the living I needed to do before having something to write *about*!

Before we were even married, Jim began to tell me I had a book in me. As our marriage stabilized and our love deepened, Jim continued to give me occasional words of encouragement to pursue my dream. A few years ago he read about a little girl, like me, who dreamed of seeing her book featured in her hometown library. More than 30 years later, she visited the library where her dream had been born, to see her book promoted on the display by the checkout desk. He cut out the article, attached a note of encouragement, and left it on the stairs where he knew I'd find it. At that time, writing a book was the furthest thing from my mind, but when I read his words of belief in me, I burst into tears. Underneath the clutter of my life at that time, Jim's encouragement fed my dream.

I recently mailed book proposals along with a few sample chapters to six agents in New York. I came home and, again, burst into tears. What if they don't like it? What if they tear it apart? Jim told me, again, that this book is good and, if they have any sense, these agents will fight over the chance to represent me to a publisher! Jim printed "<u>How to Stay Married & Love It!</u> by Nancy Landrum" on a sheet of paper. I wrapped it around a book from our shelf. He drove me to a new bookstore in our neighborhood and was glad to look foolish with me as he took a picture of me holding "my book" up in front of the store. If you're reading this, it's because it has, indeed, been published.   Without Jim's encouragement, I seriously doubt that this book would ever have found its way into your hands.

A few weeks after publication, we hosted a "meet the author" session in that same book store!

If, by any chance, you are saying to yourself, "*I'm* the one who is starving for appreciation and encouragement. Why doesn't George (or Mary) give them to *me*?" Perhaps because he (or she) is in the death throws of starvation as well.   Remember how Jim told me during our dating that he intended to love me, and love me, and love me, until my loving cup filled up and overflowed to love him back? Remember how, by *giving* respect, I *gained* self-respect?[25] Do you understand that by *giving* recognition for behavior you want, you *get* more of it back? It's a law. Somewhere I heard it called the Law of Reciprocity. The prophets of all the major religions taught some version of this Golden Rule, "Do unto others as you would have others do unto you."

Call it the Golden Rule, or Karma, or The Rule of Reciprocity—you can't consistently be a *giver* without richly *receiving* in return. None of us needs the influence of high office or great wealth to wield a great deal of power. Each of us has *immense* power to alleviate the "famine" by feeding the "hungry" around us with our words of gratitude, recognition, appreciation and encouragement. Let it begin with your SoulMate!

---

[25] Corner Puzzle Piece #3 in <u>How to Stay Married & Love It</u> by Nancy Landrum.

Puzzle Piece #6: Feed your relationship with thoughtfulness.

"I will nourish my partner and others by generously giving words of gratitude, recognition, appreciation, and encouragement."

"The deepest principle of human nature is the craving to be appreciated."
William James II[26]

"Without appreciation, a marriage will begin to shrivel, wither, and eventually die.
Everyone needs a cheerleader occasionally."
Victor M. Parachin[27]

"Kind words are like honey—enjoyable and healthful."
Proverbs 16:24

"Gentle words cause life and health;
griping brings discouragement."
Proverbs 15:4

---

[26] James, William, (August 1920). "Familiar Letters of William James II," <u>The Atlantic Monthly</u>, Volume 126, No. 2; p. 163-175.
[27] Parachin, V. M. (1995, June/July). "What Makes a Marriage Last," <u>Modern Bride Magazine</u>, page 70.

Puzzle Piece #8:

Choose SoulMate Beliefs

Chapter 6
The Soul Mate Train

"What you focus on (think about, believe) expands."[28]

I love the story of "<u>The Little Engine That Could!</u>"[29] As a child I never tired of listening to it being read. Later I read it to my own children. In that story, when a larger train engine breaks down, a little engine is asked to pull many cars full of circus animals up the hill to a town where children are waiting for the performance. It's too heavy a load for the little engine, but it keeps saying "I think I can! I think I can! I think I can!" until it finally reaches the top of the hill. It's a hero! The little engine talked itself into success.

In Book #1 we looked at the importance of *behavior* and communicating *feelings,* in building a SoulMate relationship. A vital factor that precedes both feelings and behaviors is the factor of *beliefs*.

My *beliefs* are the tracks on which I *choose* my life's direction. My choice of belief precedes the feeling-car and the behavior-car. For instance, if I choose to run on the "I am unlovable" track, I will *feel* unloved, and will *act* in such a way as to drive love away or reject it as undeserved. If I choose to run on the "good marriage is a factor of luck—if I marry the 'right' one I will be happy" track, the chances are I'll feel hesitant to commit to anyone for fear the "right" one may still be out there. The behavior that follows that belief will be avoidance of or retreat from commitment.

---

[28] Davis, Michele Weiner, (2001). <u>The Divorce Remedy</u>, p. 111. New York: Simon & Schuster.

[29] Watty, Piper, (1930).   <u>The Little Engine That Could</u>! New York: Platt & Munk Publishers.

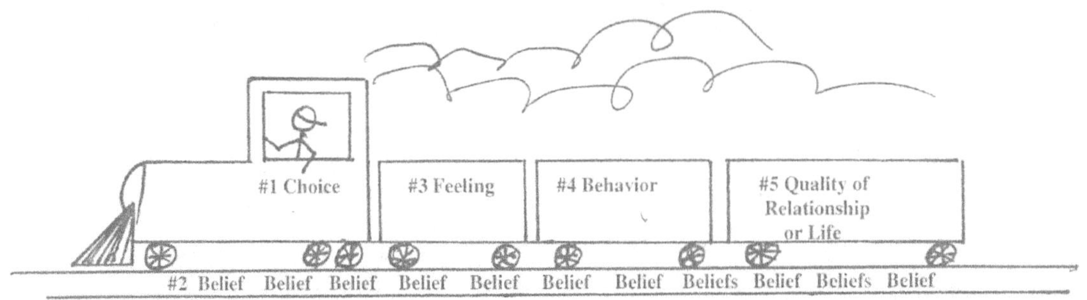

There is a big difference between *believing* and *knowing.* When I *know* something, I *know* it to the core of my being. It is absolutely unshakable. There are *no* known data that can refute my *knowing.* "Concrete is hard and I will hurt if I fall down on it." That fact will stand up to examination for the rest of my life. When I'm 80 years old, concrete will still be hard and I'll still hurt if I fall down on it. That is something I *know.* I *know* I have given birth to two children, both boys. I *know* my husband is Jim.

I originally believed many concepts to be just as irrefutably true as "concrete is hard." I didn't realize that the information at my disposal was limited. In other families, other towns, other parts of the world, there were additional facts that, if I knew them, would cause me to believe differently. For instance, my father did not like taking vacations and, once in the car, would hardly stop for anything. If my mother wanted to take a photograph he would grumble, not stopping at all or making the stop an ordeal. From my experience with him, I believed (an assumption based on limited information) that all men disliked travelling and resented being asked to stop for a photo.

On our honeymoon, we drove up the coast of California. It was April and the hills were bright green. We frequently passed gorgeous fields of wildflowers. I finally got up my nerve to timidly ask Jim if he would stop the vehicle so I could take a photo. I was shocked when he cheerfully answered, "Sure!" My belief was not changed so easily, however. I thought that after we'd been married awhile he would revert to the *true* male behavior of grumbling. We've been married more than 20 years and, so far, he enjoys vacations just as much or more than I do, and always answers, "Sure!" when I ask to stop for a photo!

Because of this new information, I have *chosen* the belief track of "some men don't like to travel and some do. Some men resent stopping for a photo-op, and others don't mind at all." I changed to a new belief track because of new information. The new belief allows me to *feel* comfortable asking Jim to stop. I'm not afraid of upsetting him.

The more experienced I become, the fewer number of things I *know*. *Personal or observed experience* is what fuels the Belief Train. I have many beliefs. I am no longer strongly attached to my beliefs, however, because I've had the repeated experience of needing to change a belief when exposed to new information. Beliefs *can* be changed—*must* be changed in order for one to grow as a person or change the quality of life or relationships one experiences.

Circumstances can be changed without changing a belief. I can change spouses, jobs, or cities, but without a change of belief, the same issues will come up with the new spouse, the income and my satisfaction from the new job will be roughly the same, and a city is just a place—it cannot essentially change me. If I want the true experience of my life to be changed, I must change my beliefs.

Young children are belief sponges. Child development experts accept as unquestionably true that foundational life-beliefs are absorbed into the unconscious before a child reaches the age of five years. Relatively few beliefs are taught through words. They are accepted as true based on personal experiences, unconscious assumptions, or "caught" by osmosis from the beliefs of those closest to us. Many beliefs are generalized to be true about everyone, in spite of the original information coming from a limited few.

A child begins developing the ability to think rationally at about ten to twelve years of age. Rational thinking is the ability to evaluate information and decide whether or not it makes sense. From that age on we have the ability to look at *new* information and use our rational thinking to evaluate that information. Most of us, however, never go back and examine the *old* data on which we based our beliefs before the age of five. New beliefs are constructed on the foundation of the old, unexamined beliefs.

Allowing my beliefs to remain unconscious—never pulling them out for close examination—is like boarding a train without any idea of where it will take me. My beliefs about men, women, marriage, conflict, love, sex, and aging . . . all determine the direction of my train and dictate my emotions and behaviors, therefore the quality of my experience of marriage.

> "To try to change outward attitudes and behaviors does very little good in the long run if we fail to examine the basic viewpoints (*beliefs*, my word) from which those attitudes and behaviors flow. Each of us tends to think we see things as they are—that we are objective. But this is not the case. We see the world, not as it is, but as we are—or, as we are conditioned to see it. When we open our mouths to describe what we see, we in effect describe ourselves, our perceptions, our paradigms." There *are* facts. "But each person's interpretation of these facts represents prior experiences, and the facts have no meaning whatsoever apart from the interpretation. The more aware we are of our…assumptions, the more we can take responsibility…examine…test them against reality, listen to others and be open to their perceptions, thereby getting a larger picture and a far more objective view." (Stephen Covey)[30]

The following quote was taken from a research project titled, "The State of Our Unions 2000"[31] conducted by David Popenoe, Ph.D., and Barbara Dafoe Whitehead, Ph.D., under the auspices of The National Marriage Project at Rutgers, the State University of New Jersey:

> "Despite doubts and difficulties, young men and women have not given up on the ideal of finding a soul mate to marry. On the contrary, they are dedicated to the goal of finding a lifelong best friend and kindred spirit. However, their ideals of soul-mate marriage contrast sharply with personal experience—as well as the popular culture's portrait—of married people. Many in this study have grown up with unhappily married or divorced parents. They know exactly what a bad marriage is, but they are less sure of what a good marriage looks like. Some can only describe a good marriage as "the opposite of my parents."

---

[30] Covey, Stephen, (1989). <u>7 Habits of Highly Effective People,</u> New York, NY: Simon & Schuster.
[31] http://marriage.rutgers.ed

Moreover, a number of study participants say they receive no advice or mainly negative advice about marriage from their parents and relatives."

What are your chances of participating in a happy, successful marriage if you believe that marriage is hard, painful, and impossible to do successfully? Not good! These experiences in childhood cannot help but create limiting beliefs about the chances of having a good marriage![32]

The encouraging news is that many marriage experts are in agreement that successful marriage skills can be *learned*, just as math or history or successful football plays. Learning the skills is important—essential—and many times, in the learning of the skills—as we experience better outcomes to our communication—our beliefs are altered, becoming more positive, more hopeful. But learning the relationship skills is just a rote exercise without power, unless the beliefs about the successful outcome of the marriage are also changed. Without the belief that you and your partner *can* build and maintain a happy, successful marriage, it won't happen. The train of your experience will follow the tracks of your limiting belief. Carl Rogers said, "In order for behavior to change, a change in perception must be experienced."

I suggest that you read this list of beliefs and check off the ones to which you have an immediate, internal agreement. After further thought, you may decide it isn't true, but usually the first response is the one that accurately reflects the unconscious belief, even though it may be in conflict with one's conscious thought.

- ❑ Women are irrational.
- ❑ Men can't be trusted.
- ❑ It's a woman's (man's) job to rear the children.
- ❑ Men are incapable of nurturing children or understanding women.
- ❑ A man who gladly helps with housework is a wimp.
- ❑ A *real* man knows how to fix things.
- ❑ A woman who dresses attractively is looking for an affair.

---

[32] Review Chapter 4 in "How to #1". The illustration shows how our beliefs are formed by the totality of our experience and, without new information, those beliefs limit our point of view.

- Now that we're married I no longer need to court, or be courted.
- Marriage means the romance is over.
- The husband (the wife) should know how to handle money.
- Women (men) can't be trusted with money.
- I am undeserving of a great marriage.
- Anyone who loves me must be a loser!
- A man can never do enough to please a woman.
- If I let myself really love him (her), I'll be abandoned.
- Conflict in a relationship means the love is gone.
- Disagreements are bad and must be avoided at all cost.
- I prove I love him (her) when I am jealous.
- A good fight clears the air.
- I can't trust him (her) with my deepest longings.
- A person is either lucky in love, or not.
- A "good" woman takes care of her man.
- If I love someone, I'll be abandoned.
- Long-term relationships are boring.
- If I am intimate, I'll lose my freedom.
- I'd be rejected if I am truthful about myself.
- I don't need love.
- If he/she loved me, he/she would know what I need.
- If he/she doesn't give me what I need, he/she doesn't care.
- If I lose you, I won't survive.
- In disagreements, one of us is wrong, one right. I don't want to be wrong so I fight to convince you I'm right.
- If you are in pain, I should be able to fix it, otherwise I'm a failure.
- If I ask what you are thinking, feeling, needing, I am intruding. If I don't ask, you think I'm not interested.

The experience of marriage will be profoundly affected by any one of these beliefs or a thousand others. I hope this sample was enough to unearth one or two irrational beliefs, or to spur your awareness of a few of your own.

One of the most relationship-damaging beliefs is, "If you love me, you'd know what I want, and if I have to tell you, I don't want it and you don't love me!" This is a crazy belief! What if we said to a waitress, "If you're a good waitress you'll know what I want, and if I have to tell you, I don't want it and you should be fired!"? Saying, "I do" doesn't make me *or* my partner a mind reader! I *do* have to ask for what I want or tell him (her) what I need! Diane Sollee[33] said about this issue, "This isn't war, it's not about building an obstacle course and using camouflage—it's marriage!"

Several clients have said to me, "He (She) will never change!" Now *that* is a limiting belief! What that statement says to me is "I am stuck in these behavior patterns with him (her). I am afraid to believe that anything will ever be better. It is easier for me to live with things the way they are or leave this person than face change. I don't want to change. I don't want to work on myself. I only want him (her) to change."

You can only be in charge of yourself, only be responsible for improving your own behavior. Be sure to read Chapter 13, "Won by One," for information about the power of one who is willing to change. Do your own work. Trust that the changes in you will benefit the relationship as well.

Another deadly belief that is influencing many of this generation is that there is only one soul mate out there. I must look until I find that one person who is perfect for me. The trouble is that "soul mate" is defined as "we never have any problems, we never fight, we always feel loving toward each other, he/she meets my spoken and unspoken needs."

If this is believed, a person will feel uncertain about every relationship. Or a choice will be made at the euphoric beginning of a relationship before issues have had time to emerge. Then, when issues do emerge, which they inevitably will, the choice will be to leave the relationship. It will be thought, "I made a mistake. This isn't my *true* soul mate. The person I seek is still 'out there.' I must continue looking."[34] This belief and course of action only postpones

---

[33] Sollee, Diane, in an interview by Jon Galuckie, www.smartmarriage.com

and complicates the *process* of becoming SoulMates. Although the choice of a partner with dependable character and openness to grow is important, it is possible to *create* and *build* a SoulMate relationship with a wide range of possible candidates.[35]

Jim and I had been through several years of hell and were now beginning to experience the pay-off from all our hard work. We were respectfully and successfully working out our differences. We were sharing our feelings and needs in a way that was honoring to each other and ourselves. We were listening. We could go weeks at a time without yelling or forgetting the rules we'd established.

I began to feel anxious. I was aware of tightness in my chest, a "waiting for the other shoe to drop" sensation, but couldn't identify a cause. Things had never been better between us. Our home was peaceful, but I was jittery. For about a month I just noticed these feelings and kept asking myself "What's going on?"

Finally, my subconscious understood that I really wanted an answer and gave this explanation to me: I was used to chaos and conflict . . . used to hurting. I wasn't accustomed to peace and love. I realized that owing to the problems we experienced during the first several years of our marriage, on top of my experience as a young widow, and stresses experienced in my childhood, I had adopted this unconscious belief, "My life will always be in trauma. I will never be happy or have peace." I was feeling disturbed and anxious because my experience was not lining up with my belief!

A couple in one of our recent workshops, did a huge amount of work, and broke through into a whole new experience of loving each other. For about two months they were on a second honeymoon! Then a major issue erupted between them. Once more he is threatening to leave, and she is not sure she can stay! Their experience is not surprising if they still believe that they aren't capable of, or deserve a happy marriage! And the skills they learned that gave them a second honeymoon will only give them that on-going experience if they *continue* using those skills!

---

[34] Study Chapter 15, "Ultimate SoulMates," to thoroughly understand the choices that *create* a SoulMate relationship.

[35] Re-read Book #1's Chapter 3: Acres of Diamonds.

If I hadn't known how to examine my feelings and look for beliefs, I might, also, have created a new issue with Jim and gone back to my old fighting techniques—just so my experience would be in alignment with my belief, as the couple mentioned above did! Fortunately, I decided to change my belief, instead. For several weeks, whenever I was aware of feeling anxious, I said to myself, "I've worked hard to learn new ways of relationship. It's O.K. to have a peaceful life. It's O.K. for me to be loved. It's O.K. for me to have a good marriage." Gradually the anxiety dissipated, and I was able to relax into the happiness that we now enjoy.

When we moved into this house, the hill in our back yard was mostly covered in weeds. I pulled out all the weeds and planted purple lantana ground cover. For the first two years, I still had to do a lot of weeding. By the third year, the lantana had spread out and covered the bare patches so no sunlight could directly hit the soil. Weeds can't sprout or grow without sunlight. Now I rarely have any weeds to pull. The lantana has usurped the weeds.

"Planting" a new belief is much the same as planting that lantana. I identified a belief that wasn't producing the relaxed relationship I wanted. Finding the culprit is a lot like yanking out a weed—you expose it as something you don't want in your relationship landscape. Just as it won't help to yell at a weed, "Don't grow there!" it doesn't help to say, "My life won't be in trauma anymore!" (That statement would actually reinforce the unwanted belief.) Instead, I consciously formulated a new belief that I thought would give me the result I desired and "planted" it by repeating it over and over, just as I regularly watered and nurtured the lantana on the hill.

If you've read any self-help books or gone to self-help seminars you've heard about affirmations. An affirmation is nothing more than the statement of a *consciously chosen belief*. The job of the train's engine—our conscious mind—is to choose a healthy belief-track on which to travel. The unconscious mind believes whatever it's frequently told. If I've lived for thirty years telling myself that my life is always going to be in trauma, my unconscious mind believes the message because it's heard it several thousand times. I didn't consciously say those words aloud. They were being unconsciously repeated in my head. In order to change beliefs, I must send a new, deliberate message to the unconscious, sometimes over and over, until the new belief takes root and overpowers the old one.

At one time I was afraid of *all* strangers. That belief led to my feeling nervous in any public place. I found it hard to respond to a friendly comment in the grocery store, for instance. I changed my belief by repeating many times over several months, "Most people are safe and interesting. I am trusting my intuition to warn me if I need protection." As that new belief took hold, without conscious effort, I began saying relaxed, spontaneous, friendly things to total strangers or responding to their comments with ease and warmth. I've experienced that most people *are* safe and likable. On a very few occasions, I've known I was in possible danger and taken appropriate steps to insure my safety. The feeling of safety followed the new belief, crowding out the feeling of being unsafe and guarded.

Beliefs that affect the marriage need to be exposed and examined. Is this belief helping me get the relationship I want? Or is it poisoning the relationship, creating a result that is hurting me or the one I love?

When we were newlyweds, Jim occasionally said, "Every time I feel especially close and loving, you crack a joke or hurt my feelings." I protested, "No, I don't!" After hearing this comment a few times over the first year, however, I decided to observe myself. It was true! I was afraid of intimacy. I thought (believed) that if Jim got too close and really saw me, he wouldn't love me anymore. At my core, I believed I was unlovable.

Although Jim's loving words, acts, and reassurances helped, they weren't enough to completely change my belief, so a few years ago I chose this affirmation: "I am joyfully receiving all the loving that is given to me and I am very loved." I said that affirmation to myself often. In addition, I made a cassette tape of affirmations, including that one, and listened to it nearly every day for several weeks. Soon I realized that I was *feeling* more loved. The feeling car followed the engine/choice of a new track/belief. I *am* lovable! Now, when Jim says to me, "I love you," sometimes I just grin and answer, "I know!" He laughs. I laugh. It feels good.

Don Juan[36] stated it this way, "We maintain our world with our internal talk. Not only that, but we *choose our paths* as we talk to ourselves." (Italics mine.) We actually talk ourselves into going the direction we're going—taking the track we're taking!   If we talk to ourselves *unconsciously*, then we are allowing our lives to be governed by those *unconscious* directives, producing *unconscious* results. Those results may be circumstances or a quality of relationship that no one would ever want!

One of the unconscious results is that we tend to attract to us the persons and circumstances that support our beliefs. This is why a woman may repeatedly become involved with men who are emotionally unavailable or a man may repeatedly be attracted to women who scorn him. Also, we also tend to dismiss or ignore data that disproves our beliefs. If I believe that men are not capable of nurturing children, chances are I'll either marry a man who is uncomfortable with children or discourage my husband from participating in any nurturing activities with our children, thus creating the circumstances that support my belief.

How do you identify a belief? By tracking backwards from the (5) quality of relationship to the (4) behavior to the (3) feeling to the (2) belief to the (1) source (previous experience) that prompted that choice.   The husband is the subject of this example, but, of course, the wife has her beliefs, as well.

Example:
5. *Quality of Relationship*: We rarely resolve conflicts.
4. *Behavior*: I contribute to that issue by my behavior. Every time my wife brings up an issue that she wants to discuss, I throw up my hands and walk out.
3. *Feeling*: When she brings up an issue, I instantly feel harassed and over-whelmed. I also feel trapped—my heart is racing and I must get away.
2. *Beliefs*: Some beliefs that might bring about my feelings and subsequent behaviors are:

---

[36] Casteneda, Carlos, (1971). A Separate Reality; further conversations with Don Juan. New York: Simon and Schuster.

All women are nags and don't deserve to be heard. Whenever a woman wants to talk about an issue I'm going to get clobbered. This will turn into a terrible fight that I can't win. I will lose control and say or do something I'll regret.

Out of those choices, I recognize this is my this belief: "Whenever a woman wants to talk about an issue I'm going to get clobbered."

1. *Source of the choice*: My mother nagged me incessantly. I couldn't do anything to please her. I always felt inadequate and powerless. I wanted to get away, but was too young to escape.

Certainly this belief-example is a direct result of a very real childhood experience with *one* woman. Avoiding the inevitable issues that arise in any marriage, however, is not a behavior that will contribute to a healthy relationship. Is it rational to believe this about all women just because it was true of one? Did I unconsciously choose a woman who would reinforce this belief? And are my current behaviors contributing to the outcome of messy, unresolved issues? Must this continue to be my experience now? Am I still choosing to feel powerless? What do I want *now*? And what do I have total control over?

5. *Quality of Relationship*: I want our issues to be resolved fairly and quickly.
4. A *Behavior* I could contribute: Whenever an issue comes up, it would help if I would immediately say, "Let's talk about it," and either immediately sit down to talk or make a date to talk as soon as possible.
2 The *Feeling* that would facilitate that behavior: A sense of safety. I would feel safe if I were confident that we could actually resolve our issues respectfully, *and* that I can call a "time out" if our discussion gets out of hand.
3 The *Belief* that would likely engender those feelings and behaviors is:

"I am willingly respecting myself and my wife. I am deserving of a great marriage and I am eagerly doing my part in creating one." I remind myself that I am no longer a child and this is not my mother! The new belief is in the form of a positive affirmation.

1. I *consciously choose* that belief over outdated beliefs that do not apply to my present life. I consciously choose the new belief "track" *every time* I am aware of experiencing the feelings or behaviors of the old belief "track." (Like planting and nurturing lantana to make it impossible for the previous weeds to flourish!) Eventually the old belief withers away from lack of reinforcement and the new belief is strengthened by frequent use.

Let's examine the affirmation in this example:
"*I am respecting . . . deserving . . . doing*"

The most effective affirmations begin with "I am," plus an active, imaginative verb ending in "ing." The "ing" ending to the verb conveys that it is an action that is *presently true and continuing to be true in the future,* such as "respecting," "deserving," and "doing." The reason that verb-tense is used is because the unconscious mind will only act on it if it believes it to be true *now.* Therefore an effective affirmation is stated as though it is presently true, although the feelings and behaviors may not be evident as yet.

"I am *willingly* respecting . . . *eagerly* doing"

The adverbs "willingly" and "eagerly" trigger in me the sense of being glad to participate in the process of working out an issue. The phrase, "respecting myself and my wife" assures my subconscious that I am no longer a victim—I treat my wife *and myself* with dignity. I am an adult, capable of participating as an equal in the working out of an issue. I am mature enough to call a "time out" if either of us gets out of control.

"I am willingly respecting *myself and my wife*. I am deserving of a *great marriage* and I am eagerly doing my part *in creating one.*"

It is important to choose words that get a positive emotional response from *you*—words that trigger the feelings and imaginary outcome that *you* want. The words that communicate success to me, may not have the same emotional connection for you.

Remember to make the statement about what you *want*, not what you *don't* want. Notice I didn't suggest "I will not feel harassed and run away when my wife needs to talk about an issue." Neither did I mention having issues to resolve. You don't want to program into the subconscious that you're going to have issues. The ultimate goal is not that you work out issues but that you have a great marriage!

Repeat the belief often for as long as it takes for the belief to take root. Put copies of it on your bathroom mirror to say to yourself morning and evening. Tuck a copy in the visor of your car to read during red lights. Give a copy to your wife and ask her to hand it to you with a hug and a smile so you can read it before she tells you that an issue needs discussing. That's a creative way to "prime" your new belief to go into action at the appropriate time.

Recording affirmations on a cassette tape is a painless, easy way to "program" them into the unconscious. It's possible to fit 20 to 30 affirmations onto a 3-minute continuous play tape normally used for answering machines. Turn it on at bedtime and let it play until waking. The subconscious never sleeps!

The feelings that go with the new belief may not appear immediately. For a while—the time depending on the length of time you've held the old belief and the depth of the evidence associated with it—you may momentarily experience the old feelings. The engine is where the power resides, however. In the same amount of time it takes a computer in the switching yard to change a train from one track to another, you can use the power of conscious choice to switch from one belief to another. If you find your thoughts wandering down the old track of "harassed and want to run," you can instantly *choose* to switch to the new track of "willingly respecting myself and my wife." It only takes a quick reminder of the new belief, along with a deep, calming breath, to transfer your train onto the new belief track. As you experience some successes resolving an issue with your wife respectfully, the subconscious will quickly deepen the roots of the new belief.

With a little experience, you'll be able to actually sense the change in your body as you "switch tracks" from the old belief to the new belief. Each belief pulls behind it a feeling or cluster of feelings. Each feeling produces the release of particular chemicals in the body. The track of "harassed and needing to escape" will produce the results of fear—adrenaline, and associated tense muscles, knotted stomach, dry mouth (no talk, just action), and shifting eye contact. The track of "willing and confident" will produce the results of calm— relaxed muscles, quiet stomach, saliva for speaking, good eye contact, warm facial expression.   Those are just the immediate *physical* reactions.

The emotional results of the new belief track will be greater self-confidence and self-respect . . . a sense of satisfaction for having overcome a handicap . . . and the pleasure of making a significant contribution to a relationship you treasure. In addition, the change in you will probably trigger a positive change in your partner. Rather than a very frustrated spouse with a list of unresolved issues, and a mediocre relationship, you are now experiencing fewer issues, issues successfully resolved, greater trust, and a wife who is glad she married you! A change in the behavior of one often brings about a profound change in the quality of the relationship.[37]

In a *consciously* lived life, the engine of the train actively *chooses* the track on which to run, rather than *unconsciously* travelling on old, unexamined tracks. I have thoroughly walked you through this one belief change. Now, use the Belief Change Exercise as a guide to identify a belief that limits your experience of marriage, and choose a belief that supports and facilitates the development of a great partnership!

We can all learn something from "The Little Engine That Could." We can each use our powerful engines of conscious thought to choose the track of "I think I can! I think I can! I think I can!" until we experience the SoulMate relationships we desire.

---

[37] You may find Chapter 13, "Won by One," encouraging!

Puzzle Piece #8: Choose SoulMate beliefs.

"I am *consciously* choosing beliefs that create and
sustain a SoulMate marriage."

**If I continue to believe what I've always believed,
I'll continue to feel as I've always felt.
If I continue to feel as I've always felt,
I'll continue to act as I've always acted.
If I continue to act as I've always acted,
I'll continue to get what I've always gotten.
Source Unknown**

"Awareness by itself is not enough: it must be joined by mastery.
We need gradually to develop a steering ability to keep ourselves
from slipping mechanically into (an old track.) We can have more
choice.
It is the difference between being impotently transported by a roller
coaster and, instead, driving a car and being able to choose which
way to go and for what purpose to make the journey."
Piero Ferrucci[38]

"A prudent man checks to see where he is going."
Proverbs 14:15

---

[38] Ferrucci, Piero, (1982). <u>What We May Be</u>, page 51. New York: G.P. Putnam's Sons.

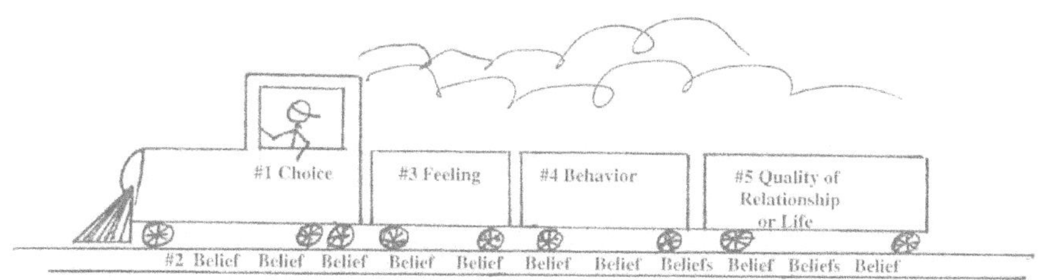

Belief Change Exercise

1.   Choose one recurring issue in your marriage.
2.   Identify one of *your* behaviors that contribute to the recurrence of that issue.
3.   In what circumstances does this behavior typically show up?
4.   What feelings precede or accompany this behavior?
5.   When have you felt those feelings in the past?
6.   What were the circumstances and who was (were) the person(s) involved?
7.   Identify the belief (or beliefs) that produces those feelings.
8.   What persons or circumstances have you experienced in the past that have supported that limiting belief?
9.   Do you want your experience to be different?
10. What is the outcome you want to facilitate in your marriage?
11. What behavior on your part would support that outcome?
12. What are the feeling(s) that, if you felt them, would help to elicit that behavior?
13. In your estimation, what belief(s) would help to create that feeling and behavior?
14. Formulate a short, easy to memorize affirmation representing that new belief.

"I am ___(energizing adverb)___ ___(inspiring verb ending in "ing")___ (plus the outcome you want to produce.)"

15. Put copies in places where you can see them, and repeat the affirmation often. If you have several different affirmations, or if you want to hear the same one repeatedly, consider making a cassette tape to listen to as you go to sleep at night. Get a 3-minute continuous feed tape (the sort used for answering machines) so you can listen to it all night. Your subconscious never sleeps! The more often it hears the new message, the quicker it will be believed, and

the sooner the feelings and behaviors will follow that facilitate the new experience you desire!

Note: Choosing a belief that will produce the feelings and behavior that you desire is the essential part. Identifying the limiting belief (steps 2-9) makes formulating the replacement belief easier, but is not absolutely necessary. Continue the rest of the process, consistently repeating and reinforcing the new belief. It will eventually replace the old one, even if the old one isn't specifically identified.

Caution: Do not try to change too many beliefs at once. That would create chaos in your subconscious. Choose the 1-5 beliefs that, if changed, would make the biggest difference in your feelings and behaviors in this relationship.

Chapter 7

Do I Have To?

**"Refusing to forgive is like drinking poison and
expecting it to kill someone else."
Source unknown**

This may be hard for some of you to hear, but I'm going to come right out and say it. No beating around the bush. It's true. There are many small and sometimes humongous events that require forgiveness in the process of creating a SoulMate marriage. Even if you think you don't need this chapter, please read it anyway. If you believe your spouse's offenses don't deserve forgiveness, read it anyway. Even if the whole concept of forgiveness makes you want to puke, read it anyway. You may be in for some surprises...

First, you may ask, "Why is this chapter included with the puzzle piece of SoulMate Beliefs rather than the ones (in Book #1) on anger or commitment?" Because the reasons we refuse to forgive or ask for forgiveness are based on our beliefs about what forgiveness is, what it does for the offender, and what it means to the forgiver.

Some misconceptions about forgiveness:

- Forgiveness is something you give when you are too weak to deal out more appropriate consequences.
- Holding onto anger protects me from further offences. Without anger, I am vulnerable. My un-forgiveness insures I will not be hurt again.
- Reminding him (her) of past offenses keeps him (her) from repeating them.

- Forgiveness invalidates the pain I've suffered, making me less important than the forgiven one.
- Forgiveness lets the offender off the hook.
- Forgiveness gives the offender the opportunity to repeat the offense.
- Forgiveness robs the offender of the opportunity to learn from his (her) choices.
- If I don't administer punishment, the offender may believe there are no consequences to his/her actions.
- Forgiveness is given only after the offender is sorry and asks for it.
- Forgiveness is something given to the offender.
- Forgiveness is an emotion and I don't "feel" forgiving.
- Forgiveness happens in a single moment of time and continues forever.
- I don't have to forgive because I would never do anything "like that."
- Forgiveness is only required if you're religious and I'm not religious.

Some truths about forgiveness:

- Lack of forgiveness (long-term anger, bitterness, and desire for retaliation), blocks the path to personal and relationship growth and damages my health.
- Forgiveness makes room for better things in my personal life and in my marriage, so forgiveness is a precious gift I give to *myself.*
- Stubbornly holding on to blame and anger sometimes mysteriously attracts the repetition of similar offenses, even from unrelated sources.
- Forgiveness is not an automatic pardon for the offender from the consequences of the offense.[39]
- Forgiveness is not an invitation to continue abusing. Forgiveness and the administration of justice are two separate and *compatible* concepts.
- Forgiveness is a powerful act of self-liberation. It is taking control of my life rather than leaving it in the hands of my

---

[39] Review Book #1, Chapter 4.

abuser.   Refusing to forgive allows the offender and the offense to remain a powerful negative force in my life.

❑ There are natural consequences that come with every offense.   Whether or not I personally deliver punishment, the offender will "pay" those consequences.

❑ Forgiveness is given for personal benefit whether or not the offender assumes responsibility for the offense or asks for forgiveness.

❑ Forgiveness does not eliminate the hurt feelings or devastation from the offense.   Those feelings still deserve appropriate acknowledgement, comfort and time to heal.   Appropriate venting of hurt feelings and being compassionately heard is often a first and necessary step in being able to forgive.

❑ Forgiveness and setting protective, appropriate boundaries for safety often go hand in hand.

❑ Forgiveness can be a single act or a process that requires strong intention, a great deal of personal commitment, and on-going work.

❑ Forgiveness is not a feeling.   It is an intention—an act of the will.   The *feeling* of forgiving usually follows, but sometimes doesn't.

❑ Although, for many, forgiveness is part of following a spiritual path, it is, first and foremost, a self-honoring part of mental, physical and emotional health for the offended one.

❑ Forgiveness acknowledges that I, too, am, at times, an offender.   If I want my offenses to be forgiven, I must forgive.

❑ The ultimate forgiveness, and sometimes the most difficult to give, is the forgiveness offered to one's self.

So how do these *truths* work out in real life?

Although neither Jim nor I had trouble forgiving the little offenses, (we were well aware that we both did annoying or thoughtless things that needed the daily sweep of forgiveness) we were both challenged by the greater, over-all forgiving of the pain we each had experienced.   After we were enjoying the benefits from our new communication skills; after we'd set up and were abiding by some rules for our marriage that worked for us; when we'd gotten to the place where we could go a week or more without a flare-up that required a mirroring session; when peace and loving were the norm, a sneaky form of bitterness began to invade my feelings for Jim. He never openly or crassly said so, but by little glimpses of his attitude, I knew he held me primarily responsible for the enormous conflict we suffered. I was perfectly willing to assume my half of the blame, but I didn't think it was fair for me to be dumped with eighty percent or more of the responsibility. When asked, he openly admitted that, from his point of view, he was the lesser offender.

Now what? How important was it that we equally share the blame for a situation that was over? Must his viewpoint match mine in order for us to move on? Was I willing to create another issue in a marriage that was still trying to recover from years of conflict? Could I "win"? Would it be worth it? What if he never saw it differently? What if, as long as we both lived, he believed that I was the primary reason we went through so much pain? My inner two-year-old (see Book #1, Chapter 14), was shouting, "This isn't fair! Stand up for me! He's being self-righteous! He needs to accept responsibility for his share!"

Fortunately, by that time, I had learned a lot about the management of frustration and other feelings. I heard my inner two-year-old, validated and comforted the feelings by saying to myself, "You're right. It's not fair. I believe that half is your fair share of the blame. But I also choose to build on the success we are enjoying rather than get stuck trying to force him to accept my point of view." Jim has a saying from his Oklahoma background that seemed to apply in this situation: "You can whup a skunk but it ain't worth it." I decided to not let those two-year-old feelings dictate the future of a relationship Jim and I had worked so hard to save. I decided that living with the awareness of his inequitable division of responsibility was a small price to pay for the otherwise great relationship we were building. In essence, I decided to forgive his judgment of me—let it go—not hold it against him.

For me, this was a process of the "unfair" feelings coming up, listening to them, comforting myself, and deciding, again, to let it go. It happened over and over again for several months. The frequency of this inner dialogue gradually decreased, until, a year or so later, it was rarely even a fleeting thought.

Four years went by without us ever discussing the division of blame. The subject of our troubled years was so painful we could barely refer to it without tears coming to our eyes. We continued to use the good tools we had learned and were enjoying the precious treasure of a loving relationship. We were not conflict-free, but were so determined to protect the marriage we had saved that we would immediately begin the mirroring process[40] whenever a hurtful issue arose.

Jim suggested that we pull all the skills together that had been the most helpful for us and teach them to other couples. I typed up a workbook of sorts and the first workshop was scheduled in just a few weeks. We had agreed that we would only share personal examples that were cleared by both of us. Our highest priority was to make the teaching of this workshop safe for our marriage.

One night after the lights were out, I asked Jim if, before we bared our souls to couples in the workshop, he thought it would be useful for us each to tell the other, from our respective points of view, what happened? It was not my intention to revive my old insistence that he see it my way. I just thought it would help us to keep each other safe in the coming public forum if we had a clear, up-to-date perspective. Jim agreed.

Very, very carefully, using the "I feel…" and "From my perspective…." language we had learned, we each shared what had happened that nearly destroyed our love for each other. There was a soft anguish in the space between us. We held hands. Tears came. The deep grief we'd both suffered was aired. I heard a change in the way Jim described his experience.   I said, "I'm hearing something different from you tonight than I've heard in the past. It sounds as though you are assuming more responsibility for what happened in our marriage than you have previously. Is that accurate?"

Jim answered, "Yes. In the past I blamed you more than me. I guess it was just unbearable for me to look at what I had done that contributed to all the pain that we and our children experienced. I

---

[40] Review How to #1, "The Looking Glass."

couldn't face it. I'm so sorry I dumped most of it on you. I was equally to blame. Would you forgive me?"

"I forgave you a long time ago, but it sure feels good to hear those words. Thank you for telling me," I answered.

In this instance, Jim needed time to heal the enormous wounds that the trauma of our conflicts had left before he could bear to acknowledge and forgive *himself* for his share of the responsibility. The recognition of his part in the pain, the forgiveness of *himself,* and finally, asking for my forgiveness, were all part of a process of healing that took place over four years. If I had insisted that he come to this place on my schedule, another painful issue would have blocked the healing we both so desperately needed. It was enough that he was working with me to rebuild our marriage. Serendipitously, we eventually arrived at the same point of view.

Adultery is, for most, the greatest violation of trust a marriage can suffer. Until I met Jim and Patty, I could not conceive of a marriage recovering from adultery, let alone building a much better relationship than before.

At the time of this interview Patty was an executive secretary for a large credit union and Jim was a pastor. Infidelity is rarely simple so I asked if they could identify some things that led up to it.

They share:

Patty: "Jim continues to tell people that he was part of the problem...not attentive enough...but I don't believe that. He was busy, but he was always attentive and we had a good love-life. After having Jason and Katrina I got back into shape and began getting nice compliments at work. For a while it was innocent, but then I began to look forward to them from certain men and thought, 'This isn't hurting anyone' so I began flirting back.

"If someone had just asked me to have an affair I would have said, 'No way!' but gradually I began justifying the attention and began blaming Jim... 'If he made more money I wouldn't have to work and be subjected to all this attention.'

"I was raised in a Christian home and had this idea that if I stepped over the line God would strike me with a bolt of lightning. When there were no immediate consequences, I thought I was getting away with more and more."

Jim: "It's sort of like gambling...the worst thing you can do is win! Even though the odds are against you, you want more. And during those years there were some really tough stresses going on. I was nearly killed in a serious car accident and needed several surgeries and a lot of care-taking. Katrina got sick at six months of age and nearly died. Plus all the normal stresses of living. The stresses added to the pleasure of escaping into these flirtations."

Patty: "During those years we moved often so my job location would change. In order to forget the previous lover, I had to find a new one. It sounds awful, but I became this awful person.

I'm especially embarrassed because they all knew I was pastor's wife! I was still attending church and being the "pastor's wife"   but the more I got away with, the less I cared about the moral laws I was breaking and the betrayal to Jim. I finally told God, 'I'm not going to listen to You anymore, I'm not going to pray to any more, I'm turning my back on you.'

For the next 1 ½ years I didn't feel guilty—but then, and I believe everyone gets to this point with any addiction—I finally hit bottom. I just couldn't deal with the inner conflict anymore. I saw two options: (1) suicide and (2) telling Jim everything so that he would be so angry with me he would kick me out. I just couldn't leave on my own."

Jim: "Patty left a sticky note on the mirror one day before she left for work...that's how I found out. I called her and said, 'We need to talk.' I left the kids at her mother's and we talked for three or four hours. I asked Patty to tell me everything..."

Patty: "...and I gladly did! I was so mean and blunt, but I wanted him   to make me leave.   Instead he said, 'I understand if you feel you   need to go, but I want you to know that I love you more   now than I ever have and I don't want you to go.' I was so   angry because he wasn't doing what he was supposed to be doing! And he added, 'But if you do go, the kids and I are going to be fine.' And I knew that was true.

"So I decided to stay and stop the affairs but insisted on this condition: 'You have to promise me that you'll never throw the past in my face.' He promised. He was never ugly or vindictive or anything so I naively thought, 'He's a pastor. He's asked God to help him forgive me.' So I didn't realize the depth of his pain and the incredibly hard work he had to do...and keep doing...in order to really forgive me."

Jim: "We talked about all of this a little off and on but not in great depth. I changed my behaviors that had contributed toPatty's hunger for attention. I called her at work more often—   not to check up on her but to just tell her I loved her and see   how her day was going. When I could I met her for lunch. I made sure we scheduled regular date nights. I did what I   needed to do to make sure our relationship was a higher priority than my job.

"And also, there were certain places I just couldn't let my thoughts go. I prayed often for the strength to resist dwelling on imaginations that would only keep the pain festering and focus my attention on the marriage I knew we both wanted.

"Then about six years later some friends of ours were going through the same thing. Patty and I agreed to be vulnerable and expose our own experience and journey with them. They found our openness to be so powerfully helpful that we decided to become a sharing couple for Marriage Encounter and then formed a support group in our church for marriages in crisis."

At the time of this interview Jim and Patty had been a pastor/sharing couple for the California Friends Church Marriage Encounter three times per year and were the founders and primary support for the weekly group, "Hope for my Marriage" for eight years. If I were to think of one word that describes their marriage, I would choose the word "grace." Their lives and their marriage are permeated with grace from above as well as grace given and received toward each other. I can't even guess how many lives, besides their own, that have been immeasurably blessed by their demonstration of the power of forgiveness.

Forgiveness doesn't always mean that the marriage is saved, however. You may remember I mentioned my sister, Sally, in Chapter 3 of Book #1. She's given me permission to tell more of her story here. It's a story that spans more than forty-five years.

Our parents were reared in an era when the male and female roles were more clearly defined than they are now so there is no blame attached when I say that their four daughters were expected to marry men "who would financially take care of" them. The woman's role was to be a good cook, a good housekeeper, become a mother and take primary responsibility for the rearing of the children.

Sally embraced their standards and expectations thoroughly when she fell in love with Ted, a man that met their approval. He was handsome, charming, fun-loving, athletic and they shared the same religious backgrounds and standards.

In spite of experiencing the usual marriage upsets their relationship appeared to be stable. They mourned the loss of their first son and celebrated the birth of three daughters and another son. As the years passed there were some cracks in the structure that, in retrospect were red flags. There was an imbalance in their parenting roles. Sally found herself struggling to teach and discipline without support, while he was the fun buddy. In other areas, she assumed more and more the role of the responsible one…the one who followed through on commitments. In subtle ways, she was designated the "problem" in the family and he was the "good guy."

Things may have gone along like this until death parted them, but Ted experienced, what to him was a life-altering disappointment in his profession. As a result, they moved to a different community and left behind the moorings of their church.

Sally began a search for greater understanding of spirituality. Ted found solace in alcohol and affairs. He became less and less available to the family. The worse things got in their relationship, the harder Sally tried to fix it…making more efforts to achieve a greater level of "perfection", trying in any way possible to avoid the painful feelings of abandonment both of herself and the family. She did everything she could to hold the family together while Ted was spinning out of control.

After several years she was physically, emotionally and spiritually depleted. After thirty-five years of marriage, she left.

After years of trying to save the marriage, she now undertook the daunting task of trying to save herself and to give her children the support they needed as they each dealt differently with the condition of their father and their family. Always a seeker, she now sought a path of forgiveness, dignity and healing by asking, "What can I learn from this experience?" More than once I heard her voice her intention to really learn how to love…love herself, love her children, and even her Ex!

In his way, he regretted the problems he'd created, at one point sending Sally a note asking for her forgiveness for all the pain he had caused. Sally responded honestly, "I find (forgiveness) to be somewhat complex. If it means letting go of the past, finding peace in the present, and hope for the future, then I can honestly say I have accomplished huge chunks of that."

It wasn't a quick and easy task, but eventually she was able to invite her Ex to family celebrations and holidays. They had occasional moments of quiet reflection about the years they'd shared and the family they'd created. Ted praised Sally for being a constant in the lives of their children.

As his health deteriorated due to alcoholism, one of his daughters did an intervention. He responded by going into a treatment program at the local Veterans' Hospital. After only a few days there, he died quietly in his sleep during an afternoon nap.

He was financially destitute, so, again, out of concern for the needs of their children to remember their father, Sally paid for a burial, and a beautiful memorial service where a variety of friends and family remembered his humor, his earlier accomplishments and expressed compassion for his struggles.

Sally's journey began when she chose to remove herself from being the victim in an abusive relationship. It continued with her driving need to make meaning out of the wreckage of her marriage and led to a deeply profound *process* of forgiveness, not only of her Ex, but of herself; learning to forgive *herself* for the ways she had abandoned herself and her own needs, hopes and dreams. She is known by all as a caring, loving, and compassionate woman who chose to turn the rocky soil of her life into a beautiful and peaceful garden. I feel honored to call her my sister and my friend.

All of the above is about *giving* forgiveness. The other side of the forgiveness process is *asking* for it.

Some misconceptions about asking for forgiveness:

- Asking for forgiveness makes me too vulnerable. My "softness" will be taken advantage of. The offended one will expect me to assume all responsibility for any problems we have.
- Asking for forgiveness makes me look weak. Admitting I was wrong will cause him (her) to lose respect for me.
- Asking for forgiveness will invite "punishment" from the one I've wronged.
- I'm not fully responsible. I'll ask forgiveness when he (she) does.
- Admitting I'm responsible for any part of our problems is simply too terrifying. Once I ask forgiveness, I'll be expected to change. I don't know if I can.
- I believe that what I did is unforgivable.
- Words are cheap. I'll prove I'm sorry by changing my behavior.
- Asking for forgiveness is a manipulative way of getting out of trouble.
- Asking for forgiveness means I must resume full relationship with this person and I would rather not.
- The offended one must be alive and willing to see me in order for me to ask forgiveness.

Some truths about asking for forgiveness:

- Admitting wrong and asking for forgiveness exposes our humanness, allowing another to see our fragile underbelly of vulnerability to mistakes, poor choices, and deliberate hurtful acts, but that vulnerability often strengthens the resolve to change a hurtful behavior. It is often the first step on the path of change.

- ❑ Asking for forgiveness is an important part of assuming responsibility for developing emotional intimacy. When emotional intimacy has been hurtful in the past, it may be hard to "drop your guard."
- ❑ Any person who genuinely wants a relationship with you will appreciate and respect you more for admitting when you've been hurtful and asking for forgiveness.
- ❑ Asking for forgiveness is something you do to respect yourself, regardless of how it is received by the offended one. Therefore,
- ❑ Ask forgiveness for your own integrity, even if the other party refuses to accept their responsibility for hurting you or refuses to forgive you.
- ❑ You're only responsible for your part of the process. You have done your part to bring about reconciliation when you ask forgiveness. It's up to the other party whether or not they choose to forgive.
- ❑ Asking forgiveness is separate from resuming intimate relationship. Some are not safe persons with whom to be close. The choice of whether or not to be involved in an ongoing relationship is a separate one from giving or receiving forgiveness.
- ❑ Asking forgiveness is manipulative only if getting out of trouble is your motive for doing it. Only you know your heart.
- ❑ Nothing is unforgivable. Forgiving yourself is essential for moving forward.
- ❑ Because asking forgiveness is essentially something done for one's own mental and emotional health, it is possible to ask a trusted "stand in" for a dead or unavailable person to hear your request for forgiveness. Guideposts and Angels Magazines[41] occasionally share stories of departed loved ones sending signals of forgiveness from the other side.

---

[41] www.Guideposts.org/Angelsonearth.

How to do it:

"I realize I hurt you when I ___(name behavior). Or, "I was wrong when I ____." Would you please forgive me?" Simple, isn't it?

Please note: (this is *very* important!)

If you offer any excuses or reasons why you did _____, the request for forgiveness is invalidated! No excuses, even though you may think there were contributing circumstances!

The offended one may need time to forgive. Or, may grant forgiveness but it takes time for good feelings to return. Or, forgiveness may be granted, but some guidelines for future behavior need to be worked out so the offended one is reassured that the hurtful behavior won't reoccur. Forgiveness is often a process rather than an event on both the giving and the receiving sides.

We have both found that the toughest forgiveness to give and receive is forgiving oneself; and the toughest self-forgiveness for us by far, has been forgiving ourselves for the pain we inflicted on our children. All of our children have experienced the loss of a parent in addition to the usual assortment of insecurities and disappointments suffered by most of us in the process of becoming adults. The years of conflict between Jim and me often distracted us from the needs of our children, and added to the burden with which they had to cope. Three of the children have established responsible, adult lives and successful families despite the lacks in our parenting. We each have a son, however, who chose drug abuse to relieve his internal pain.

Our journey with these two sons has taxed us to the limit of our understanding. We've alternated between anger at them for their destructive choices, and loathing for ourselves for not, somehow, preventing this waste of their intelligence and potential. In the beginning of these journeys with drug-addicted children, we had all the usual misconceptions. We thought we could control them. We believed we could fix it. We looked for answers and sought programs and bailed them out of the messes they created.

It's a long, long story of an even longer process, but the bottom line is that we felt responsible. We made so many mistakes. We disciplined too much—or not enough. We gave them too much help—or not enough. A good parent would have seen trouble coming and stopped it. Good parents would have solved their own problems faster so that the needs of the children would be their foremost concern. Good parents wouldn't have children with drug problems. Therefore, we decided, we are bad parents. We failed at the relationship in which we wanted most to succeed. Their struggles are our fault.

The self-imposed label of "bad parent" has to be, for some of us, the most devastating judgment of all. Over a period of years, however, we realized that judging ourselves as bad parents contributed nothing toward a solution. In fact, when *we* assumed responsibility for their choices, we made it harder for *them* to be responsible. The shame we felt for their drug dependency blurred our ability to relate to them in ways that supported their recovery. We eventually grew to recognize that drug dependency is a very complex problem that does not lend itself to simplified answers or solutions. As we gained more experience, and perspective, we realized that it is impossible to completely identify which parts of their susceptibility to drug addiction came from our choices as parents, the fractures in our society, the influence of peers, their physical or genetic pre-dispositions, and the individual choices they made about how to cope with their inner wounds.

Gradually we saw self-judgment as an insidious enemy of healing—both ours *and* theirs. We began the work of forgiving ourselves for judging ourselves as "bad parents." The process of this forgiveness-work has been, at times, grueling. As we have whittled away at our harsh judgment of ourselves, some comforting truths have emerged. *We* do not see ourselves as products of *our* parents' values, ideas, or choices; therefore, it's unfair to see our children only as products of us. They are individuals with gifts, weaknesses, and lessons to learn just as we are. Although we have the responsibility to give our children the best foundation in life for which we are capable, we do not have the power to guarantee that they will have the lives we want for them. There is a profound element of personal choice as well as other factors beyond our control.

As our journey of self-forgiveness continued, we accepted full responsibility for the ways we had hurt our children and asked their forgiveness; but we relinquished responsibility for their adult lives to each of them. Anything less would be disrespectful of their power as adults. One of the boys said that he experienced a great sense of relief when handed full responsibility for his choices. The other has repeatedly said that his choices are his alone . . . that we have no responsibility for the decisions he's made.

Moving to an even higher perspective, we believe that our understanding of life is faulty due to incomplete information.[42] We are only equipped to see things from a human point of view. How can we know what purposes are served from an eternal point of view? We believe that each person comes into this life with certain lessons to learn, and, with our limited understanding, what right have we to judge that this path is better or that path is worse for learning those lessons? We also believe that *no* path is beyond the unconditional love of God.[43]

If one of the lessons that Jim and I were sent here to learn was the lesson of self-forgiveness, we were given the perfect sons to facilitate that lesson. Dare we believe that we were the perfect parents for whatever lessons they were sent here to learn, as well? In the course of our marriage recovery, we've come to see, with profound amazement, that we each chose the perfect spouse to help us learn what we longed to learn, and desperately needed to learn, about loving. In the learning we were challenged to overcome many of our weaknesses. Believing in a mysterious design that is ultimately perfect requires trust in a universe designed to support our welfare.

Nevertheless, when the attacks of self-judgment hit, both of us still go through the routine that, now, is so familiar.

- ❑ I place my hand over my hurting heart and say, "I forgive myself for judging myself as a bad parent. The truth is I did the best I knew how to do every day." I may repeat this several times, focusing on allowing the balm of forgiveness to penetrate the hard knot of self-blame.

---

[42] See Book #1, Chapter 4, "A Different Point of View."
[43] My son died of congestive heart failure after 15 years of drug addiction. Jim's son is currently sustaining a "clean" recovery after years of struggle.

- ❑ I remember that this child made choices I would never have encouraged. I give him the respect due an adult, allowing this person who is separate from me to learn his own life lessons from the consequences of his choices.
- ❑ I release him to the loving care of God.

Bouts of self-blame are less frequent and the healthy detachment (not disinterest or lack of love) that is an essential part of having a healthy relationship with adult children has become easier to maintain. Chapters 8-11 more thoroughly explain the role that codependence has in relationships with addicts. Sally's story in this chapter might be identified as a powerful story of recovery from codependence for a woman married to an addict.

Summary:

Both the asking and the giving of forgiveness are first, and foremost, something I do for my own mental and emotional health. Refusing to forgive allows the offender to continue to occupy a position of power in my life. The original offense keeps offending, often exerting control over aspects of my life. The offender continues to occupy an important place in my consciousness which may act like a magnet attracting the very qualities in my behavior or attitudes that I despise in him (her).

Refusing to ask forgiveness prevents me from experiencing myself as a person of integrity. If I can't face and accept the "dark" qualities in myself, they'll not be available for me to change. In regard to someone I love, the refusal is a barrier to a better, closer relationship.

Both giving and receiving forgiveness is a SoulMate choice.

Some further tips on Forgiveness:

Mary Ortwein, author of *Mastering the Mysteries of Love* relationships skills program, emphasizes the need to first create physical, psychological and relationship safety. That means determining to use respectful speaking and listening skills (mirroring) when dialoguing with the other person involved. The boundaries of those skills reduce the possibility of increasing hurt and anger.

She goes on to say, "There may be situations (with each other or with others) when safety may include physical separation, an extended cooling off period, the presence of a third person, or even the imposition of legal processes. Forgiveness does not mean accepting abusive, violent, dangerous, or manipulative behavior. It does not mean putting self or others in danger. Even legal action against an offender does not work against forgiveness. All create safety. Forgiveness must stand on a platform of safety and cannot begin until physical and psychological security is achieved."

And here are some pithy quotes by Michael Beckwith, pastor of Agape International Spiritual Center in Los Angles from his *Life Visioning Workbook*:

"All victims have a blame story. As victims, we create these stories to explain how someone or something else is responsible for our present circumstances. We use them to justify why we can't move forward, and we expertly argue down to the finest detail how these stories prove that our point of view is correct. In short, it's not our fault: they are to blame.

"The practice of forgiveness, when offered unconditionally, will heal you. The word 'forgive' means to give up a claim to requital; it means to relieve someone of debt to you. In spiritual terms, when you forgive, you release someone or something of their responsibility for your happiness. You forgive not to heal someone else, but to heal yourself.

"Here is your forgiveness practice: Identify each individual to whom you attach a blame story. (And this individual may be yourself. NL) You might say, 'What you have done or not done cannot determine my happiness or my destiny. I set you free from blame and I set myself free through the power of forgiveness.' …you are releasing your own unforgiving thoughts in order to free yourself. The work is not easy—it takes courage. It is a labor of the spirit that will set you free.

"You're deciding not to give your power away to anyone or to any circumstance, incorrectly believing they determine your success, your health, your happiness, or your wholeness. You're stepping into a greater sense of empowerment by taking responsibility for your life."

Puzzle Piece #6: Choose SoulMate Beliefs

"I courageously choose to ask forgiveness when I am at fault,
and graciously forgive,
so that I can experience the best of who I am,
and enjoy the best possible relationship with the one I love."

"Only he who never sinned may throw the first stone!"
John 8:7

"...and forgive us our sins,
just as we have forgiven those who have sinned against us."
Matthew 6:12

Puzzle Piece #9:

SoulMate Responsibility

Chapter 8

Velcro?

**"You can't make trouble for others
without a little of it rubbing off on you."
Unknown**

Velcro used to be an oddity but now it's used to fasten jogging shoes, wristwatches, windbreakers and even pillow covers. It's that bristly stuff that has loops on one side and tiny little hooks on the other. When they get anywhere near each other the hooks grab the loops and hang on. When you pull them apart it makes a tearing sound, as though something were being shredded.

Several years ago I hired a carpenter to build some cabinets in my sewing room. The first few days he was diligent and made quick headway. Then several days went by when I didn't hear from him. I called. He said he'd gotten another job and would get back to finish mine in a few days. I just said, "O.K."

On the day he said he'd be coming, I stayed home all day, waiting. He didn't show. I expected him to call with an apology and explanation. He didn't call. After a few days *I* called *him*. He apologized, explaining that he'd been "busy" with a new job, and would come "for sure" next Thursday. Thursday came and went without a word. This pattern continued for *9 long months!*

For awhile, I complimented myself on being so adult, willing to wait in line. I thought a good person was always patient and kind. I thought being understanding was very loving of me. As this scenario was repeated many times, however, complete with his excuses and my patience, I began to experience an inner crisis. I was beginning to feel angry! I wanted my sewing room finished! As is often true with important life lessons, I didn't know that he was doing me a big favor.

My resentment grew and the pressure increased. I didn't want to be mean, but clearly, what I was doing wasn't working. His irresponsible behavior was forcing me to reevaluate my belief about what it meant to be kind. How could I maintain my commitment to being a loving person, a value that was important to me, and cope with someone who was taking advantage of me?

After pondering this dilemma for several weeks, I had a burst of insight. I realized that I was participating in his irresponsible behavior by meekly agreeing to it. This was *not* a loving, kind or genuinely helpful way to be. Making it easy for him to be irresponsible was, in fact, unloving! I was not acting in a way that was of higher integrity at all. I was an equal participant in an unconscious scheme to be negligent!

Like a child closely examining a new toy, I turned this amazing idea over and over in my mind, checking for any flaws. Finally, I was ready to call him. I quietly asked, "When is the first possible day you could be finished with my job?" He answered, "Next Wednesday." I replied, "In that case, for every day after Wednesday that my job is not finished, I will subtract $20 from the balance I owe you."

He was incensed! Didn't I know that he had to support himself? Other, bigger, better paying jobs had come along! He would get around to mine when these jobs were finished! Why couldn't I be patient?

I respectfully (lovingly) answered, "You contracted to do my job *before* you contracted to do these others. I've been patient long enough." I repeated, "For every day after Wednesday that my job is not finished, I will subtract $20 from the amount I owe you." *He* slammed the receiver down. *I* smiled. That was Saturday afternoon.

On Monday morning he pulled into my driveway with a helper in the passenger seat of his truck and my cabinets in the back end. *He* was so furious he wouldn't speak to me or look at me. *I,* on the other hand, was no longer angry. I was calm and a little amused. By late afternoon, the cabinets were installed. In spite of the nine extra months it had taken to get it done, I paid him the full balance.

It was a cheap price for a very valuable lesson. He helped me see "loving" from a completely different point of view. Why did I think being forever kind to him was admirable when the price was being neglectful of my own needs? My "patience" meant I was supporting *both* of us in our irresponsible behavior. I now understood that, by taking my stand with him, I was actually caring for him by giving him a strong incentive to honor his word. I was also caring for myself, refusing to continue being his doormat. I felt liberated! Long before I'd ever heard the term, I had just experienced my first lesson about *codependency*.

Why did the cabinet ordeal last so long? Because my Velcro hooks of wanting to be "loving" grabbed onto his Velcro loops of wanting patient compliance for his irresponsible behavior. We danced the codependent Velcro dance for nine long months. Who knows when my cabinets would have been finished if I hadn't decided to get off the dance floor, ripping apart the Velcro bond by loosening the grip on my dysfunctional definition of loving!

I believe the core of codependency is a misunderstanding of the meaning of love. The carpenter obviously thought that I should passively co-operate with whatever he wanted—have unlimited understanding for his "good reasons." I believed that love was patiently shouldering the burden of the consequences of his irresponsibility—the non-completion of my job and his repeated lying.

In Book #1, Chapter 14, "Me? A Two-Year-Old?," I briefly described a theory of relationships suggesting that the chemistry attracting us to one another comes from a deep, instinctual intelligence in our unconscious. One aspect sometimes included in this phenomenon is the hooks and loops attraction of codependency.

Jim: "My comments are for you guy-readers. For many years I dismissed the term, 'codependent' as psycho-babble. It is hard to understand. The term itself seems to be a misnomer. When Nancy wanted to include a section on codependency in the book, I thought, 'Oh, no! These are going to be chick chapters!' Don't get me wrong. I had experienced the benefit of weeding codependency out of our marriage and was convinced that exposing and disconnecting from codependency in a marriage could be, and often is, an important step toward a SoulMate relationship. I was hesitant to include a section about it in the book, however, because I couldn't imagine very many guys sitting still for a codependency lesson.

"As this section of the book developed, I would read it to see if it was 'male friendly.' Codependency is a slippery concept. I was relentless in my insistence that the explanations be clear and logical. So she re-wrote it again and again and again. She's succeeded. I believe these chapters to be the clearest explanation of codependency and its effect on relationships that I have ever read. I sincerely believe that if you will stay engaged and give this carefully written section a fair hearing, the benefits to all your relationships will be rich!"

"Co" refers to the truth that it takes *two* persons voluntarily participating for a codependent relationship to exist. Both persons are irresponsible in different ways. (The whole relationship doesn't necessarily have to be codependent. There may be areas of the relationship that work very well and other areas that don't.) "Dependence" refers to each person depending on the other for the things described in the next few paragraphs.

Two distinct kinds of behavior, one with hooks the other with loops, come together for the codependent dance. On the one side of the relationship a person will act irresponsibly. From now on I'll call him "Irry," short for "irresponsible." (I'm making Irry a "he" for the sake of simplicity. Irry may be either male or female.)

He will, perhaps, be late for work, refuse to balance his checkbook or pay his bills on time, thoughtlessly leave messes, procrastinate with projects, blame others for his feelings, or practice an addiction to alcohol, drugs, gambling, raging, sex, work or spending. In areas where he is irresponsible, he treats his partner with disrespect, disdain, or blithe indifference and demonstrates thoughtless disregard for the consequences of his choices.

Irry is often charming, masterfully enlisting others to clean up his messes. Or Irry may be pitiful, enlisting sympathetic assistance. Most of the time, whether by being charming or pitiful, someone agrees to pick up the slack. Although the procrastination was his, the secretary will work overtime preparing his presentation to important clients. A parent will bail him out of legal or financial problems. Credit card companies continue issuing credit to him, in spite of his poor credit history. His wife will pick up his dirty laundry, used dishes, or soda cans, assume primary responsibility for the parenting of his children while forgiving, or at least tolerating his thoughtlessness, neglect or cruelty.

One who assumes Irry's responsibilities or rescues him from unpleasant consequences is called an "enabler." For ease of this narrative I'll call her Abby, short for "enabler." (I'm referring to Abby as a "she" although this role, as well, may be assumed by either gender. Sometimes these roles are traded back and forth in the same relationship.)

Irry *depends* on Abby to intercept the uncomfortable consequences that would otherwise be the natural result of his irresponsibility. Irry is also *depending* on Abby to help keep him unconscious of his dysfunctional life. As long as there is an Abby around, he needn't face all the ways his life isn't working very well. He may ignore the consequences of drug or alcohol addiction until his body or his life falls apart. He may pretend his addiction to pornography, gambling, or excessive spending, isn't hurting anyone—it's just a little fun in his life. Irry may delude himself into believing that his long hours at work are because the job demands it, or he needs the money or promotion "for his family." As long as Abby tolerates his irresponsibility, lack of good balance, negligent, demeaning behavior, or physical abuse toward her, she supports his belief that "It's for her own good," or "This is just the way I am," or "I can't change," or even, "You're the problem, not me!" Irry usually *depends* on a whole cadre of Abbys to keep him unconscious of his irresponsibility, support his otherwise unbalanced life, and provide someone to blame when he is unhappy.

Abby is also unconsciously *depending* on Irry for some very vital things, as well. She *depends* on him to give her life a sense of purpose. Her purpose is to love him, which really means "save" him by patiently forgiving his faults and cleaning up the messes he leaves in his wake. Often she experiences a self-satisfied righteousness as she "helps" him. If she is successful in making *his* life run smoothly then *her* life has meaning. She feels important. Abby is *dependent* on her success as his rescuer to convince herself that she is a good person, deserving of love.   Deep in her heart she believes that in exchange for all the sacrificial things she does for him, she will be loved.   It may take a long time for Abby to wake up to the reality that he didn't agree to that exchange. She will never feel loved in the role of enabler.

In addition, she is *depending* on his dramas to keep her distracted from her own low self-esteem. As long as her energy and attention are used for saving *his* life, she can justify neglecting the work she needs to do in order to take care of *her* life. If she is focused on providing what *he* needs, she is exempt from the hard work of figuring out and getting what *she* needs.

Abby often feels exhausted, overwhelmed and resentful. That should come as no surprise. She also feels ashamed, guilty, and disillusioned.   Abby feels ashamed because at some level she knows she is compromising her own integrity, and at times, hurting others or even breaking the law in order to protect Irry. The level of dishonesty may be profound as she attempts to convince herself she is happy and loves him while Irry's behavior continues to drain her of self-respect. She feels guilty, because no matter how much she does for him, she is failing to make him happy or his life good.   She is disillusioned, because she thought "saving" him would make her life meaningful, but instead, it feels wasted. As codependency runs its course, Abby feels hopelessness, despair, and profound bitterness. In essence, Abby has abdicated responsibility for her own life, feelings, and welfare.   Codependency, therefore, is a disease of mutual, interlocking irresponsibility.

The two persons who make up a codependent relationship find each other like the hooks and loops of Velcro. They stick. They fit. Each partner practices patterns of behavior that strengthen and support the dysfunctional beliefs and behaviors of the other. They end up feeling trapped and resent or even hate each other for the dance they co-create. Irry is angry because Abby didn't "fix" him and Abby is enraged because all of her inner resources have been used up without receiving the love she thought would be the reward. In the long view, neither person gets what they really need.

As long as they both believe that this is how their needs will be met, however, they have very compelling reasons for keeping this "Velcro" arrangement going. Both persons remain stuck in patterns that make it easy to blame the other for his or her unhappy life. As long as Irry can blame Abby for not helping him enough, or letting him down when he really needed her, or keeping his life miserable with her unhappiness and demands for love, he can avoid the painful awareness of his own culpability. He sees himself as Abby's victim rather than looking at his lack of self-responsibility. As long as Abby can blame Irry's negligence or abuse for her unhappy, unfulfilled life, she doesn't have to look at her voluntary participation in the relationship. She sees herself as his victim rather than acknowledging that she has abandoned her life to the control of another.

Inevitably, co-dependency begets blame. With blame, the solution to unhappiness remains "out there" in the hands of another person or a change in circumstances. This point of view keeps one perpetually a victim of things beyond his or her control. Blame, resentment, depression, guilt, shame and defensiveness are just a *few* of the results of this pattern.

> "Co-dependence is fostered when two people unconsciously agree to be the partners in each other's dramas. An unconscious bargain is struck: If you won't make me change my self-destructive patterns, I won't make you change yours. If you will let me project[44] my childhood issues onto you, I'll be the target for yours. The trouble is that co-dependence feels so bad that people start complaining shortly after the dramas get under way. At that point, we start to blame our troubles on the other person."[45]

------

[44] See Chapter 10, "Going to the Movies."
[45] Hendricks, Gay & Kathlyn, (1992). <u>Conscious Loving</u>. Page 7-8, New York: Bantam.

At the time of the sewing room saga, my education in codependency had only begun. I was too attached to being thought of as nice and caring. I needed love and approval from others too desperately and was too unsure of my own worthiness to give up my codependent ways so easily. I honestly didn't see most of the ways I was participating in codependent relationships. In the years since, I have identified myself as both Irry and Abby at different times—in the same relationship or in different relationships.

I once had a friendship with Jill. At the beginning of the relationship I probably was Irry. I hadn't been a widow long. I was still trying to recover some balance. Jill and her husband were so kind, warmly welcoming the boys and me into their lives. We spent a great deal of time with them. With hindsight, I believe I handed them a big chunk of the responsibility for helping me to heal and for sharing some of the heavy responsibility for two little boys. Jill, in particular, rearranged her life around our needs, and I willingly accepted the huge commitment of time and energy she gave to us.

Years went by. I became stronger. I was ready to assume more responsibility for my life. I began to venture out from the protective umbrella of Jill's friendship. I didn't want to lose her as a friend, but I wanted more friends. I also wanted to find a man with whom I could share my life; but whenever I had any contact with someone new, or enjoyed an event without her along, she was threatened and suspicious. She would demand all the details. Who did I talk with? Where did I go?

I began to get frequent lectures about how I was letting her down. She had been a friend to me when I needed her, and now I wasn't being a friend to her. I believed her. I had switched roles and was now Abby. I wanted to be a good friend, so I kept trying harder—and feeling more resentful. After a few dates with a man for whom I really cared, the whole issue blew up. She wanted me to stop dating him. She didn't think he was right for me. She didn't trust him. I was caught between trying to be a good friend and wanting to move forward with my life. I eventually consulted a respected neutral party for some perspective, because I was so afraid I *really was* a bad friend.

I decided to ask Jill for some time off from our friendship—time to regain our balance as individuals. I know my request was devastating for her. I hurt knowing how much I was hurting her. Our friendship never recovered. I accept full responsibility for the codependent, Velcro roles I played that kept us locked together in a way that was ultimately, devastatingly hurtful to all of us. It was a very painful lesson.

Later, when I ranted and raved at Jim or the children, I was Irry. I was unconsciously asking them to suffer the consequences of my irresponsible anger. I wanted them to act certain ways, do certain things, treat me a certain way so that I would feel loved, successful—a good wife and mother. When they didn't do what I wanted, I blamed them for my unhappiness. While justifying my behavior as being "for their own good," I was really asking *them* to be responsible for convincing *me* that I was successful as a wife and mother.

While periodically exploding at Jim or the kids, I was also demanding super-human efforts from myself in this quest for the perfect life, perfect family. Something had to give. I became so depressed I could barely get out of bed. I developed insomnia. I began binge eating in secret. I gained a lot of weight! I found a counselor who specialized in eating disorders. Fortunately for me, she understood the root cause to be a combination of over-responsibility for others in an attempt to win love coupled with an under-responsibility for my own welfare. The conflict had created a volcano of such frightening feelings that I had driven them underground. Those powerful feelings had erupted as an eating disorder.

I was encouraged to journal as a safe outlet for my feelings.[46] In addition she gave me permission to ease up on my excessive responsibilities for others while learning to be more responsible for myself. At first, I couldn't believe that recovery could come by being *less* responsible! I was terrified! Wouldn't I disappoint or even damage those I loved if I backed away from taking care of them? ("Them" included Jim, the kids, the boss, the business, the house,

---

46 Review Book #1, Chapter 12, "Finding the Treasure in Anger".

the parents, et al.) Mightn't our lives just crumble if I didn't keep everything running? I believed that I needed to sacrifice myself in order for the needs of those I loved to be met and in order for me to be loved. I was afraid that if I made decisions in support of my own wellbeing, someone I loved would be neglected . . . or possibly the world would end!

It doesn't require strict religious training to adopt a credo of loving others at our own expense, but some of us may have learned this faulty principle of relationships in church. The victim definition of "love" may have been actively taught or might have been my misunderstanding stemming from my own fragile sense of self-worth. I thought that loving another person at great sacrifice to myself would make me godly. Then, perhaps *God* would love me and give me many brownie points. When my counselor pointed out that the Bible said I am to "love others *as you love yourself*," it shocked me.[47] In the years since, I've come to the conclusion that it is only possible to genuinely love another person *to the degree I love myself.* Anything else might appear on the surface to be love, but is probably an unconscious bid for approval, value, meaning or love.

I've also come to believe (and, so far, every experiment has proved it to be true) that when I make a decision that is *authentically* based on what I *know* to be healthy for me, it is automatically healthy for anyone else involved, as well. (Others, like the carpenter, may or may not be *happy* about my choice; that is immaterial.) The universe was not set up so that what is healthy for one is damaging to another . . . God is much smarter than that!

I prayed for a situation where I could experiment with being a *little* irresponsible without hurting anyone. Just for practice. Two weeks later I was buying groceries. I picked up a carton of yogurt, and somehow, between the shelf and my cart, it slipped out of my hand. Splat! The lid flew off and blueberry yogurt spread out in a three-foot wide star-burst pattern! I stood there looking at it for a minute, then burst out laughing, and walked away! Did you get that? I just walked away! How irresponsible!

I knew someone would report it to the manager, but this time, it wouldn't be me! Someone would be paid to clean it up. It didn't

---

[47] Thank you to my wonderful lay counselor, Jackie Barrile!

have to be me! Accidents happen. I decided not to grovel in apology to the manager repeating "I'm sorry" over and over or grabbing a mop and cleaning it up myself. I walked up and down the aisles, finishing my shopping, with a grin from ear to ear. I must have looked a little ditsy! I didn't care! It was a giant step for me to take. I felt liberated! I didn't have to hold the whole world together by my excessive sense of responsibility. That silly escapade gave me hope.

Gradually I learned to let go of responsibilities that weren't really mine and relaxed my grip on the consuming fear of being imperfect. I began to love myself rather than attempting the impossible task of making others prove my love-ability. I still remember the sensation of an enormous weight lifting off of me when I was told that just because there was a job that needed doing, I didn't have to do it! Slowly, I was becoming more responsible for *myself*.

The conflict that is inevitably caused by a Velcro relationship, while undoubtedly being a source of pain, *is also holy ground*. It is the place where I am challenged to learn, to grow, to heal. It involves much more than simply changing a pattern of behavior. It is changing my beliefs about myself—what will make me valuable, lovable, and worthy or give me self-respect. It's also changing my beliefs about the other person—what is truly loving, respectful and in the best interests of him or her.

It is not easy work! When I play the role of an enabler in a codependent relationship, I believe that I am valuable only if I am nice, do whatever is needed, have a child who is "good," or earn another's approval. Deciding that I am lovable just because I am and choosing to believe that I am valuable simply because I am a human being takes a leap of faith for dedicated enablers. Knowing that I am worthy of fair treatment, a peaceful existence, a good life, nurturing relationships, or reasonable expectations is half a world away from thinking I am worthy *only* if I can perfectly please everyone in my life.

Experiencing feedback from our behavior is the primary way we learn.   Allowing others, especially those I deeply love, to suffer the consequences of their own choices, is the ultimate act of love for them and respect for their life-learning process. Interfering with that process is robbing them of the opportunity to grow. When I do that, I unknowingly communicate my lack of confidence that they are capable of learning what they need to learn in order to have a decent life. I participate in crippling them rather than loving them.

To be sure I'm understood, I add this disclaimer: The consequences must be age appropriate. It is not appropriate to allow a six-year-old to walk home in the dark, or send a teen-age daughter on a date with a stranger, or expect a twelve-year-old to understand the consequences of jumping off a bridge into unknown water. A six-year-old could experience the consequence of going to bed early because he wouldn't get out of bed in time for school that morning. A teen-age daughter could be expected to suffer the consequence of missing a mall-date with friends because she didn't clean her room when asked. A twelve-year-old can survive going to school in dirty clothes since he didn't do his laundry after being taught how to do it. After the age of 18, assuming there's no mental impairment, everyone has the *capacity* to logically think through probable consequences to actions. Therefore, both legally and morally, we can be held responsible for the consequences of our choices.

Codependency is rather easy to spot when a wife is buying booze for an alcoholic husband or a dad is bailing out a chronically in-trouble son. However, it is powerful enough to erode love in a marriage when practiced in more subtle ways, as well. In the beginning years of our struggle to save our marriage, when I brought up an issue to discuss, Jim's feelings would be hurt. It was painful for him to face the reality that there were areas where I was unhappy with him. It was also painful for me to see how deeply he was hurt, and to think that I *caused* his hurt, so I would back down, in essence being irresponsible to my *own* feelings. The issue would go underground for a while, and then resurface, bigger than before. I eventually realized that, unconsciously, Jim was deflecting our attention away from a painful conversation and the possibility of dreaded conflict by being excessively "hurt." Then, I was choosing to be dishonest by pretending the issue "really wasn't that important."

We eventually realized that our mutual participation in this method of avoidance prevented us from finding workable solutions to issues, thereby increasing the amount of resentment between us. From that time on, if Jim's feelings got hurt when I respectfully brought up an issue, I was sympathetic to his feelings, but did not back down. If he needed time to deal with his feelings before resuming our "mirroring,"[48] he could take a time out, but not shelve the problem indefinitely. The "issue" would no longer magically disappear. By dropping my role as protector of his feelings and assuming he was capable of successfully managing his *own* feelings, I supported Jim's growth in this area that was critical to our marriage success. Soon, Jim gained more confidence in his ability to deal with conflict and his use of "hurt feelings" to fend off painful confrontations disappeared.

When I give up the role of "Irry," believing that I can handle the consequences of my choices and learn from them, a gigantic step into emotional maturity has been taken. Learning to be appropriately responsible for the choices I make and caring about how those choices affect those I love is a courageous act of liberation. Understanding that self-respect comes from respecting the way I conduct my life rather than seeing how far others will go to help me, gives me a firm foundation on which to build a balanced life.

A huge step has been taken when I give up the role of "Abby," (believing that I am deserving of love only by inappropriately assuming another's responsibilities.) Understanding that I have tried to control and fix another to protect myself from pain, rather than authentically helping, is a quantum leap into better mental health. Releasing a loved one to learning from their choices is a truly loving choice. Setting firm boundaries to take loving care of myself is self-honoring.

For confirmed codependents, learning to stay within the circle of our own responsibilities and use our own authentic power takes a lot of strength. I am still learning how to do it. I don't wrestle with

---

[48] Review Book #1, Chapter 9, "The Looking Glass."

the same issues I had 15 years ago, but life generously provides new issues on which to sharpen my skills . . . (smile).

Separating two persons from their unconscious contracts that support mutual irresponsibility results in a tearing apart that is often noisy, just like separating strips of Velcro. It rarely happens quietly. It's a new beginning, the birth of a healthier life—messy and painful—but a necessary step to the delight of SoulMate love.

Melody Beattie said that we take care of people's responsibilities for them. Later we get mad at them for what we've done. Then we feel used and sorry for ourselves. That is the pattern, the triangle. This list of a few characteristics of codependency was extracted from a much more comprehensive list in Co-dependent No More[49] by Melody Beattie:

- ❑ Doing something we really don't want to do.
- ❑ Saying 'yes' when we mean 'no.'
- ❑ Doing something for someone although that person is capable of and should be doing it for him or herself.
- ❑ Meeting people's needs without being asked and before we've agreed to do so.
- ❑ Consistently giving more than we receive in a particular situation.
- ❑ Fixing people's feelings. (Doing something *just* to make them feel better.)
- ❑ Doing another person's job for them.
- ❑ Speaking for another person.
- ❑ Solving people's problems for them.
- ❑ Putting more interest and activity into a joint effort than the other person does.
- ❑ Not asking for what we want, need and desire."

In the following four chapters, I'll explore some specific ways that codependency plays out in marriages as well as other relationships, and share some examples of how to separate stuck-together places so you can fully experience a SoulMate relationship.

---

[49] Beattie, Melody, (1987). Co-dependent No More, p. 42-52. New York: HarperCollins

**Puzzle Piece #5: Assume full responsibility for your
own feelings and behaviors. Allow others to be
fully responsible for their own feelings and behaviors.**

"I am willing to learn how to
separate from *unhealthy* codependence with my spouse."

**"Grandfather, Great Spirit, you have set the powers of the
four quarters of the earth to cross each other.
You have made me cross the good road,
and the road of difficulties,
and where they cross, the place is holy."
Black Elk[50]**

*" . . . and love your neighbor as you (already) love yourself."
Leviticus 19:18[51]
Matthew 5:43
Matthew 19:19
Matthew 22:39
Mark 12:31
Luke 10:27
Romans 13:9
Galatians 5:4
James 2:8*

---

[50] Neihardt, John G., (1972 edition). <u>Black Elk Speaks: Being the Life Story of a Holy Man of the Oglala Sioux</u>, p. 209.
[51] This must be a concept the writers of the Bible thought to be important as it is stated in nine different places! Every religious tradition encourages the same concept, sometimes stated in different ways.

Chapter 9

The Invisible Barrier

**"Two wrongs don't make a right,
but a fight."**

As described in the previous chapter, two persons in a codependent behavior pattern are stuck together like the hooks and loops of Velcro. While joined in this crazy dance, they are also separated by a barrier erected from the blocks of unhappy feelings created by codependence. Both analogies are helpful in understanding codependence. Resentment, blame, guilt, crippling pity and shame are a few of the blocks that build the invisible barrier. Those feelings have never been known to enhance a relationship!

Just as a wall is built one block at a time, a dysfunctional, codependent relationship develops with the use of one disrespectful response, one irresponsible or enabling act, one limiting belief at a time. As individual resentments are not dealt with in a healthy, respectful way, the wall grows. The cement gluing the blocks together into a wall is a lack of understanding about how to be healthy in a relationship or an unwillingness to do the personal work necessary to learn.

Because codependency seems to be a difficult subject to understand, and the principles hard to know how to apply, and the concept so essential to healthy relationships, I'm writing five different chapters about it. In each chapter I approach the subject from a slightly different point of view. If it's a new, or misunderstood concept for you, by the end of Chapter 13 perhaps these words will make more sense. Ultimately, it is my intention to make the concept so clear that you'll know exactly if, and where, steps need to be taken to pull apart any Velcro places in your relationship, and how to remove the blocks of resentment that are the substance of the invisible barrier between you and your beloved.

The anagram of BARRIER will help me describe the characteristics and results of codependence in a relationship. Just as with communication tools, if healthy boundaries of responsibility were not demonstrated in my home of origin, then the *concept* must be learned before healthy responsibility can be *practiced*.[52]

B BOUNDARIES BETWEEN RESPONSIBILITIES ARE BLURRED

Where there are fences between our house and the houses on either side of us, it

is easy to distinguish between the lawn that is ours to mow, and the lawns that are

the neighbors'. In contrast, the boundaries between individual's responsibilities are invisible. As a healthy adult, the things for which I must be responsible remain in my "yard" so to speak. In a healthy *relationship*, the things for which the other person must be responsible remain in the other person's yard. It's as though we each have an invisible property line surrounding us within which we "own" our individual stuff . . . stuff for which no one else can *successfully* be responsible.

There are some things that even a great partner cannot do for me. No partner can, with good results, take care of my job, my role as a spouse or parent, or assume the burden of the consequences when I am irresponsible. No partner can successfully *make*

me happy, or *make* my life meaningful, or *make* me feel loved. All of those things remain in *my* yard.

---

[52] Review Book #1, Chapter 7, "Am I a Duck or a Chicken?"

My partner may, if he or she chooses, contribute to all of those things—by being supportive, by participating in a mutually honoring relationship of personal growth, by giving me room to grow, by being flexible about life changes, by loving me in meaningful ways. All of which means that I, too, give support, honor, space, flexibility and love.

When I step over into my partner's yard, assuming responsibilities or consequences that can only, with healthy results, be assumed by him or her, the vicious dogs of resentment, defensiveness, blame, and crippling irresponsibility soon attack both of us. At the same time, the dogs in *my* yard are set off because I have neglected my own responsibilities. Each time the boundary of appropriate responsibility is crossed, a block is placed between us erecting a barrier to SoulMate love.

Besides the boundaries *between* husband and wife, there are boundaries that *encircle the marriage* delineating a healthy separation between it and all other relationships. The boundary of emotional and sexual faithfulness is the most elementary. SoulMate love cannot be experienced when one or both partners dilutes the quality of their commitment or love by sharing it outside the marriage with fantasy, pornography, or adultery.

Another way the boundaries that encircle the marriage are violated is when either partner has relationships outside of the marriage that take precedence over the needs of the marriage or marriage partner. This can happen when one turns a child into a pseudo-partner, spending time and sharing inappropriate intimacies that rightfully belong to the spouse. Friends or a job can also become substitute partners, robbing the marriage of the energy and intimacy that it needs for good health.

Of course, the reverse is also true—when the marriage becomes the be-all, end-all of both partners, excluding a healthy balance of other relationships, even to the neglect of a child's needs.

If you suspect the marriage boundaries are being violated in either of these ways, it would be wise to consult a therapist especially trained in family dynamics.

A **ADDICTION TO CONTROL AND APPROVAL** There seems to be a see-saw-like cycle to co-dependency. One cycle is *control*. I must have the house exactly so. I demand to know where you are every minute and exactly what time you'll be home. I must be sure you are not practicing an addiction. I must have you with me at all times. I must have all facets of any particular part of my life aligned just the way I want them or I'll make you pay—by either a foul mood, silence, criticism, judgment, raging, or more extreme abuse.

An obsessive compulsion to force someone else to do what I want them to do or be what I want them to be—to fit into the mold I've constructed for them—is an addiction to control, one of the symptoms of co-dependency. This may take the form of excessive worry. One of the characteristics of an addiction to control is that I expend more energy trying to force the *other* person to change than I spend on examining how *I* need to change. I spend more time in their yard than in my own!

The corresponding cycle is the need for *approval*. I will do anything to please you. I will put myself through Houdini contortions to make sure that you are happy with me . . . approve of me . . . love me. The obsessive need for approval keeps me chasing after the one who's approval I crave. Usually, with the characteristic wisdom of the universe, the one being pursued continues backing away or withholding his or her approval. It is clear that the unhealthy craving for another's approval will never bring the self-worth or love I crave.

The two halves of the cycle are saying something like, "You're not doing it right. I'll do it!" and then "I have to sacrifice myself, doing things I resent doing, in order to have your approval."

One wife in our workshop shared that she wants the house cleaned a particular way. She wants her husband to help her, but when he doesn't do it up to her standards, she is resentful. She says something like, "Oh, just forget it! I'll do it myself!" Of course her husband is less and less enthusiastic about helping since he can never please her. She realized her need to control the miniscule differences between her way and his way was damaging their relationship. She must decide between doing it her way, happily and alone, or sharing the load without such rigid standards.

A friend of mine is a whiz at getting things done, and done very well. In the office where she works, she recognizes that she has a pattern of assuming new responsibilities without relinquishing any of her current tasks. She is exhausted and often resentful because her life is out of balance. She sacrifices her energy and spare time trying to win approval and control the quality of work. Gradually she is learning to re-claim a more reasonable balance in her contributions to work and care for herself.

<table><tr><td>

R

</td><td>

RESISTANCE TO FEELINGS

</td></tr></table>

A classic symptom of co-dependency is resistance to feelings. While enabling the irresponsibility of another, I resist admitting that I feel resentful. I try to "make" myself feel happy to give. I shush my internal whispers of dissatisfaction. I shove down my anger. I hide being upset because I don't want to hurt someone. I tell myself, "I shouldn't feel this way." I make excuses for not dealing with my feelings by saying things like, "He (she) needs me," or "I can't change things, so why try."

While acting irresponsibly, I resist the feelings of shame. I defend myself and blame others for my failures. I live on the shallow surface of my feelings, reluctant to examine the low self-worth that is at my core when I neglect responsibilities that are really mine. I shove all hints of my own longing for self-respect far below the surface of my awareness.

All of these feelings are hints that something essential to my wellbeing is being ignored.

I'm also resistant to my partner's feelings. I am over-concerned about being the object of my partner's displeasure or of hurting his or her feelings. I'm afraid to speak up when I feel hurt or disappointed, so "stuff" it in order to protect my partner. A SoulMate relationship is built on truth, not pretending.

I am resistant to feelings if, when my friend is unhappy, I try to make him or her cheer up. I may move heaven and earth to help a loved one, and then feel angry when my efforts aren't appreciated.

I was picking up a prescription in the drug store. Several people were waiting in line. A little boy scratched his leg on the edge of the display and began to cry. His grandmother held her hand over his mouth whispering, "Shhhh!" over and over. She was resistant to his very normal expression of pain, more concerned with the attention that was focused on them.

Jim and I have both lost a spouse and a child. We have heard all of the things people say to the bereaved in an effort to make them stop hurting. Why isn't it O.K. to just hurt? To grieve? Why do so many want the survivor to hurry up and feel better? Because they are resistant to the feelings that come with grieving a loss and the long process involved in recovery from a great loss.

Jim conducted a funeral service for a man who had been the widow's husband for 55 years. Her son escorted her up to the open coffin after the service to say "good-bye." The old woman began to cry softly. The son said, "Now, Mother! You've done real good. Don't let me down now!" He was so resistant to feelings that he couldn't let his mother grieve the death of the man with whom she had shared her life for 55 years! [53]

<table><tr><td>R</td><td>

RESCUE OF OTHERS FROM NATURAL CONSEQUENCES
It's appropriate to rescue a child from the consequences of running into a busy street! It is not appropriate to buy booze for</td></tr></table>

an alcoholic, or bail out a repeat offender, or lend money to someone who foolishly squandered the rent money, or lie to an employer to cover your spouse's "sick day" spent fishing, or take back home an abusive spouse who has not consented to therapy, or make up excuses for a spouse who has missed an important occasion with a child, or protect a spouse from disappointment when I say, "no". Every time I step in-between a person's action and its natural consequence I am interfering with his or her opportunity to learn.

In their study of California history, 4th grade children in our state learn about the string of Catholic missions founded by Father

---

[53] Review Chapter 16, "I'm Only Trying to Help!" for ways to genuinely comfort.

Serra. When my son, Steven, was a fourth-grader, his assignment was to make a model of one of the California missions. He came home on Thursday, made this announcement, and nonchalantly added that it was due the next day.

I exploded, then stayed up until about 11 p.m. helping him finish it. I felt taken advantage of and resentful, but satisfied that he would turn it in on time. He felt lectured and ashamed, but happy that he would turn it in on time.

But what did he learn? He learned that when he procrastinated, Mom would bail him out! He was actually rewarded for being irresponsible because I helped him much more than I would have if he'd allowed plenty of time! That was not the lesson I *consciously* wanted to teach him! I had inadvertently taught him to depend on being rescued because *I* had *unconscious* needs that being the rescuer *temporarily* met.

I wanted to be a successful mother. Among other things, that meant my child would do well in school.[54] I stepped over into his territory and assumed the lion's share of the responsibility for his project. *I* suffered the consequences of *his* procrastination because of my need to look good as a mother. As a result I robbed Steve of a wonderful opportunity to learn a valuable life-lesson.

I met with a couple several times before their wedding. In the past she had caught him in a couple of relatively minor lies, things he passed off as jokes or inconsequential. Then he'd trapped himself into revealing that while on a business trip he'd stopped in to see his old girl friend, although he'd assured his fiancée that he hadn't. This soon-to-be-bride had been hesitant about the previous incidents, but this time the lie could not possibly fall into the "joke" or "inconsequential" categories. I'm not convinced that he ever really assumed responsibility for the lie or the consequence of her loss of

---

[54] Perhaps a future book will be about the tremendous burden I placed on my children to prove to the world that I was a good mother. From my conversations with other parents, I know I was not alone in using my children to salve my insecurity. It's not only unfair to our children, but dangerous to ourselves to measure our value solely on the choices made by our children.

trust. She wanted the marriage so badly that, in my opinion, she eventually glossed over the issue. If, indeed, she did do that, she left the door open for future lies and further loss of trust—more blocks in the Invisible Barrier.

A complicating dilemma arises when the consequences of your spouse's choices also cause suffering for you and, perhaps, your children. If his or her behavior may result in the house going into foreclosure, for instance, the stakes are high and the choices much more difficult. It takes amazing balance to find a way through such a tangle of difficult options. During a time like this, faith is the only place I know of to find refuge and wisdom. It may be faith in God, faith in the support of the universe, faith in yourself, or faith in the tenets of a support group such as Codependents Anonymous,[55] but faith is needed to rip apart the Velcro to gain freedom from the prison of codependency.

| I | **INEQUALITY OR INAPPROPRIATE INVOLVEMENT** |

INEQUALITY OR INAPPROPRIATE INVOLVEMENT
Co-dependency is such a complex mix of behaviors and feelings. Each of these categories is like taking a snap-shot of it from a different perspective. All of these snap-shots have places that overlap. *Inequality* could be described as a state where one person's needs are consistently more important than the other's. Inequality is also when one person shoulders more of the burden of responsibility than the other. Resentment is inevitable.

One of my clients works long hours for moderate pay, then comes home to fix dinner, bathe the children, oversee homework and bedtimes, and fix tomorrow's lunches. Her partner works part-time at a low paying job, spends a good deal of his salary on beer, and complains if dinner isn't served on time. She feels trapped because she needs what little money he contributes to help pay for household expenses, and yet she's longing to break out of a relationship that traps both of them in an unhealthy, co-dependent dance. The total

---

4. Codependents Anonymous is a nation-wide group listed in most local directories.

responsibilities of the partnership, including parenting, are unequally divided.

An incredible example of *inappropriate involvement* was reported in the newspapers some time ago. A professional athlete was very unhappy with the amount of playing time he was being given. Finally his wife went to management on his behalf. I doubt that her husband knew what she was doing. Jim tells me that no self-respecting man would welcome his wife "going to bat for him" with his employer! As soon as possible, the manager transferred this pro to the other side of the country to play for another team!

One young couple came to me in desperate trouble. She was complaining about her husband to co-workers, friends, and her grandmother, asking one and all for advice. He was moaning to his parents and siblings. I suggested that they cease all talk about their relationship other than, respectfully, with each other, a counselor, and perhaps their pastor. They chose, instead, to dissipate their energy on complaining sessions with multiple others—energy that could have gone toward the building of a successful relationship. There was nothing seriously wrong with the relationship that focused attention couldn't have corrected; yet in a few short months divorce proceedings were begun. They had invited many others to be inappropriately involved.

 ENTANGLEMENT RATHER THAN RELATIONSHIP

Many wedding ceremonies include the words, "the two shall be one..." Indeed, two persons in a highly functioning, healthy marriage seem to work together with nearly seamless unity. Isn't that what a good marriage should be? Each dependent on the other, both keeping up their end of the relationship?

Yes and no. This simple analogy comes to mind. A shoelace is a single entity, one string, united in one purpose—to hold a shoe snuggly against the foot. After being inserted in the bottom eyes of the shoe, it is divided in half. As both halves zig-zag through the eyes and meet at the top, then cooperate in the tying of a knot and bow, they successfully fulfill their purpose of being together. Although the lace is one, the two halves function independently.

If the laces become double knotted together, stuck in a tangled mess, they have lost their ability to cooperate. Now they are locked in an embrace that, rather than being loving, is more like being chained together. The discomfort of the tangled knots becomes the focus of their energy rather than the teamwork that could move them toward mutually beneficial goals.

In a healthy partnership, each half of the shoestring is being fully responsible for its job, and working in easy cooperation with the other half, who is also fully responsible for its job. There is mutual sharing, mutual responsibility, a give and take in the investment of time and attention. Sometimes the circumstances of life may dictate that one partner's needs are temporarily primary; but perhaps, at some later time, the other partner's needs may require more attention. Each is willing *for a period of time* to shoulder more of the load for the other . . . but not indefinitely. Not if both partners are well and capable.

For the first several years of their marriage, Mary wrapped her life around Sam's desires. For the most part, she did what he wanted, as he wanted it done, and when he wanted it. Lately she became aware of her growing discontent. She is beginning to back away from her excessive involvement in *his* interests and to reconnect with activities that please *her.* She remains fully committed to their marriage. He isn't happy about the change. He feels abandoned and unimportant to her. She feels trapped between resentfully doing what he wants or taking care of some neglected parts of herself.

The change is simply growth. The emotions that are being triggered are characteristics of an entanglement rather than a relationship. They are poised on the edge of devastating conflict or fantastic growth. Which way it will go depends on their readiness and willingness to be responsible for their individual shoestrings. Do they want to see the current "tangle" as an opportunity for personal growth and healthier SoulMate partnership? Then with mirroring, and perhaps counseling, they will look at options that allow for the adjustments necessary as each of them grows. By taking steps individually and together they can unknot the strings and co-operate in the process of building a successful SoulMate partnership.

R

RESULTS: RESENTMENT!

Many, probably even most, relationships begin as a tangled enmeshment surrounded by a soft cloud of romantic love and sexual energy. As stated before, the serious purpose of the relationship usually becomes apparent at some later time when the unconscious agendas of each partner begin to result in unfulfilled expectations—and (I'm sure you know this by now!) resentment.

As an enabler, my resentment comes from believing that I am a victim . . . that I am powerless. I have surrendered my power to someone else, allowing that person to dictate the quality of my life. I have chosen the role of helplessness. In childhood I may, indeed, have been safer if I feigned helplessness. For some of us, reclaiming the power to make our own choices in life requires courageous steps, often requiring the support of a counselor, trusted mentor, or support group.

Authentic personal power doesn't grandstand or berate another or explode in ways that damage or destroy. My first attempts to claim authentic power, however, were quite awkward. Those hesitant steps into self-responsibility didn't look particularly graceful or dignified; but they were a beginning—a beginning as precious and exciting as watching a baby learning to walk.

As someone who is irresponsible, I feel resentment because someone near me is not passively agreeing with my demands or putting up with the results of my irresponsibility. For some reason, it seems to be universally easier to see ourselves as the victim rather than the abuser. I resented Jim when he would walk away rather than "take" my verbal abuse! I did not want to see his behavior as a natural consequence of my irresponsible expression of anger!

It takes great courage to examine the source of resentment and evaluate the cause as my choice of being the *victim*, or my unwillingness to give up *victimizing*.

One of the most frequent by-products of resentment is *depression*. Depression often comes when resentment is "stuffed" or abusively expressed to another.[56] I was depressed not only from stuffing my resentment toward Jim, but from my disappointment with the way I was acting.

Resentment also creates *distance* in the relationship. Every time I submit to being treated disrespectfully without being truthful about how I feel, a block is added to the barrier. Every time I treat my partner disrespectfully, another block is added. Every time the truth is not spoken the wall becomes thicker.

There used to be only a few feet separating East Berlin from West Berlin, yet the distance created by the wall was impenetrable for most Berliners. When the emotional distance in a relationship seems impenetrable, some become so lonely that the marriage is abandoned in search of emotional connection rather than doing the work of removing the blocks and closing the emotional distance with the spouse.[57]

In addition, resentment gives birth to *disillusionment*. So many of the couples that come to us were children of unhappy or divorced parents. Each couple wants their marriage to work, but lacking successful role models, is terrified that it won't. When issues arise between the partners, they tend to have the resigned belief that it was inevitable. One of the most frequent feedback remarks we get after a workshop expresses gratitude that we are so transparent about the problems we've had *and* the obvious pleasure we now experience in our marriage because we learned how to successfully remove any block of resentment. After practicing the skills we teach, many couples sigh with relief because now they know they can make their marriages work "'till death do us part."

Our daughter, Teri, told me recently that now she knows that she and Greg can work anything out . . . that nothing can separate them because they have the skills and the willingness to resolve any conflict. *That* is SoulMate love! *That* is a SoulMate relationship!

Where does co-dependency erect a barrier? Co-dependency erects a ~~BARRIER~~ between me and my loved one making it impossible to experience SoulMate love. It's that simple.

[56] Book #11 Chapter 12: "Finding the Treasure in Anger," tells how to safely vent anger so it does not poison one's self or the relationship.

[57] Check out the consequences of this choice in Chapter 30.

Here's another check list to help you determine if the BARRIER of co-dependency is creating distance between you and your SoulMate.

From Gay and Kathlyn Hendricks in <u>Conscious Loving</u>:[58]
"Ask yourself whether you have some of the following issues in your relationships:

- In spite of your "best efforts," people around you do not change their bad habits.
- You have difficulty allowing others to feel their feelings. If someone feels bad, you rush in to make it better. You worry about other people's feelings frequently.
- You do not let yourself feel the full range of your feelings. You are out of touch with one or more core emotions such as anger, fear, or sadness. Anger is a particular problem for you. You find it hard to admit that you're angry. And you have trouble expressing it (appropriately) to other people.
- You criticize or get criticized frequently. You have a strong, nagging internal critic that keeps you feeling bad even in moments when you could be feeling good.
- You try to control other people, to get them to feel and be a certain way, and you spend a lot of energy being controlled or avoiding being controlled by others.
- Your arguments tend to recycle. Conflicts are temporarily ended by one person apologizing and promising to do better.
- In arguments, much energy is spent in trying to find out whose fault it is. Both people struggle to prove that they are right, or to prove the other wrong.
- In arguments, you find yourself pleading victim or agreeing that you were at fault.

---

[58] Hendricks, Gay and Kathlyn, (1992). <u>Conscious Loving</u>, p. 10-11. New York: Bantam Books.

❑ You frequently agree to do things you do not want to do, feel bad about it, but say nothing.
❑ People seem not to keep their agreements with you."

The next chapter—"Going to the Movies"—outlines a challenging, but profoundly liberating process for assuming full, appropriate responsibility for upset feelings. Chapter 11 relates real-life examples of individuals and couples who, one block at a time, have successfully broken down the Invisible Barrier of resentment. Chapter 12 describes the magic that can happen when you assume full responsibility for what you contribute to the relationship even when your partner is not interested in working on the marriage with you. The final chapter of this section gives some tips for successfully managing responsibilities within the unique dynamics of a stepfamily.

Puzzle Piece #9: I treat myself and my spouse with dignity when I allow each of us to be responsible for our respective choices.

**"A lasting, equitable solution to any issue
can be found when the approach is:
We are one. Resolving what hurts the effectiveness
of our partnership or damages our emotional
intimacy is a shared responsibility."'
Jim and Nancy Landrum**

"Treating yourself like a precious object
will make you strong."
Julia Cameron[59]

Chapter 10

---

[59] Cameron, Julia, (1992). <u>The Artist's Way</u>, New York: Putnam Books.

Going to the Movies

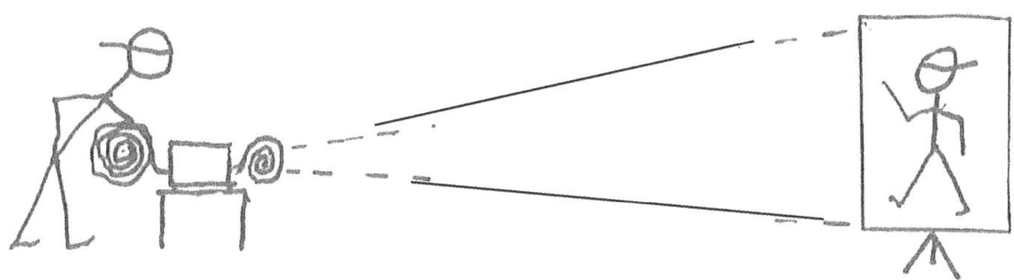

"(Marriage) is the merciless revealer, the great white searchlight turned on the darkest places of human nature."[60]

A movie projector takes a very small image on a piece of film and passes it in front of a relatively small, but powerful light source inside the projector. The light "projects" the image onto a screen. The image on the screen is a "projection."

My Webster's Dictionary definition of a psychological "projection" is: "The act of externalizing or objectifying what is primarily personal, subjective, or *perceived* rather than *actual*." (Italics mine.)

I have opinions or beliefs (images) about myself hidden inside the personal projector of my subconscious mind. My reaction to another person's actions or attitudes sometimes "flips the switch," causing these hidden opinions or beliefs in me to be projected onto a screen. The projection is what I believe or think about that other person. The screen is the person about whom I have that opinion or belief—the one who's behavior or attitude "flipped the switch." Just as with film, it is possible to have either positive or negative images projected from one's subconscious projector onto another person.

When I admire a person or ideology it is a positive projection of something similar within myself. The projection comes from an

---

[60]Porter, Katherine Anne. "The Necessary Enemy," <u>The Collected Essays</u>, p. 184.

unconscious part of me that recognizes my potential for demonstrating the very things I admire about another. My admiration is calling me to be aware of, develop, and appreciate those same things within me.

I have always had a great deal of admiration for any person who has been through trials of some kind, gained wisdom, and then shared his or her wisdom with others as a speaker or writer in a way that was interesting and challenging. My admiration for such persons was a clue that I had the capacity to be like the persons I admired. My subconscious "projector" was calling me to develop the qualities of being a life-learner, teacher, speaker, and writer. Those qualities were the images on the film of my subconscious projector that were being "projected" onto another person by my admiration. I still admire such persons, but now it is with the conscious awareness that I am one of them. When I didn't see myself as one of those persons, but admired them, it was a "projection." Now I "own" that projection, that is, I consciously recognize that my admiration comes from the part of me that, to some degree, shares those qualities.

When my reaction to another is negative, (condescension, frustration, fear, anger) my subconscious is "seeing" the negative qualities that I dislike about myself on the "screen" of the other person. If I judge what I see on the "screen" of the other person as wrong, or bad, or unacceptable, this "projection" is outer proof that there is inner rejection and judgment of myself occurring. These emotional upsets are called "negative projections."

A negative projection is taking place when some event has triggered upset feelings. An opportunity to learn and heal has been provided, yet it's not easy to take the learning/healing route. It is much easier to blame or judge others for my upsets and justify being upset "because . . . .". It is more comfortable to see the cause of my upsets as something or someone outside of myself. When I "project," my life energy is diverted into judgment, self-righteousness, hurt, and anger, and is therefore not available for loving, resolving issues, setting healthy boundaries, or being at peace.

Unrecognized and disowned negative projections are emotional baggage that dis-empowers me with victim thinking. That baggage is a magnet, attracting more and similar upsets, generously giving me additional opportunities to learn and heal.   Until consciously acknowledged, the projection continues to lurk in that part of my psyche often referred to as the "shadow"—the part of myself that I don't like, so I keep it hidden from myself to protect myself from shame and my own harsh judgments.

There are three possible reasons why I project negative hidden beliefs or opinions about myself upon another person:

1) That person or ideology[61] is doing something that I do to myself, or dislike about myself, of which I am unaware;
2) That person is demonstrating something I do to others that I disapprove of or believe to be rude or harmful, but of which I am unaware of doing;
3) That person is doing something I judge as "bad" or "wrong" that I have not accepted that I, also, have the capacity to do, given circumstances that are dire enough.

In theory, *every time I am hurt by, upset with, irritated, angry, outraged toward, or judging another person, I am "projecting" one of my own hidden qualities upon them*. I am literally seeing a part of myself that I don't like in them. Since learning of this concept, I've examined hundreds of my own upsets and, so far, the examination has always exposed some part of myself that I don't like and don't want to "own" (accept as true about me or be responsible for changing).

One of the interesting things about projections, both positive and negative, is that it is possible to project a quality onto another person that isn't even true about that person, simply because it is hidden in myself as a quality or a belief. One classic example is when a man is suspicious that his wife is being unfaithful. She may not have an unfaithful thought in her mind, but he has been unfaithful in the past or is tempted by infidelity and so he is "projecting" or seeing

---

[61] Projections can be exposed by our negative over-reaction to an idea, or group of people who represent an idea, but for the purposes of this chapter dealing primarily with the marriage relationship, I'm going to limit my references to personal relationships.

that possibility in her. A woman may be suspicious that her husband is being unfaithful simply because her father was unfaithful to her mother, so her belief is to expect betrayal from all men, including her husband.[62] Assuming he is, indeed, faithful to her, she is "projecting" her negative belief about men onto her husband and experiencing all the suffering that she would if, indeed, it were true.

One of my clients frequently accuses his wife of having an affair. As far as I can assess, she isn't. His first wife was unfaithful to him and left him. It was devastating to him. He is "projecting" the image of his unfinished business with his first wife onto his present wife. The image of an unfaithful wife is coming from the beliefs he adopted based on his previous experience, or from the unresolved anger he still harbors toward his former wife. The suspicion and constant monitoring of his present wife's every move is slowly poisoning a marriage that has been, in every other way, very good for him.

It is often easy to identify projections when we observe them in someone else. For instance, we see a father and son who don't get along and are always "setting each other off." We smile because it's obvious to us that they are so much alike. The father and son are reacting to the qualities in each other that they don't like about themselves. "Dad is so hardheaded," the son might complain. "He just won't listen to any idea that disagrees with his own!" Guess what! The son isn't listening either! And is being just as "hardheaded" about doing things his own way!

When the World Trade Center was destroyed and the Pentagon damaged, killing thousands of innocent persons, some projected their outrage by beating up, destroying the property of, or even killing persons of mid-East descent. Many Pakistanis, Iranians, Egyptians, or persons who just had dark skin were subjected to ostracism, obscene gestures, and rudeness. Prejudice is a form of projection. These acts were demonstrating the same behaviors and attitudes as the terrorists who hijacked the planes for their suicide missions. The difference is only a matter of degree. Illegal acts must be justly punished, but as one astute citizen said when being interviewed, "If we take an eye for an eye, soon the whole world will be blind."

---

[62] Review Chapter 6, 'The SoulMate Train."

Hurting or destroying innocents in retaliation for hurting and destroying innocents, only proves we are no different than those terrorists.

I may deplore the bigotry in others, yet be unaware of, and unwilling to "own" the bigotry that resides at some level in me. I may criticize a friend for not meeting the needs of her child, when my own child has needs of which I am totally unaware. I may rail at the boss for his dictatorial, rigid way of managing his responsibilities, and be blind to my own insensitive, autocratic treatment of my spouse. I may be angry with a family member for neglecting me, and refuse to remedy the ways I neglect myself.

Disowned negative projections (negative qualities I am not aware of "projecting" onto another) wreak havoc in relationships. The closer the relationship, the more deadly are the disowned projections.

In the next several paragraphs, I describe the slow exposure of a powerful negative projection in me that profoundly affected our marriage. When Jim and I married, we agreed that neither of us would try to be a parent to a step-child who was, or nearly was an adult. Jimmy, however, was only 8 years old. Jim asked me to be his mom. I gave Jimmy his choice of calling me "Nancy" or "Mom" and he chose "Mom."

Jimmy's Mama Dixie had been chronically ill all of his life. Jim had assumed, in essence, the role of a single parent. Dixie was on the sidelines enjoying Jimmy, laughing at his antics, and praising his accomplishments, but had not been well enough to bear the stress of discipline or excessive little-boy energy. That was Jim's job. Jim delighted in doing "guy" things with Jimmy—playing ball at the park, teaching him how to ride a bicycle, and roughhousing. The fun was a welcome distraction from the grief of Dixie's illness. After Dixie's death, the primary source of consolation for Jim *and* Jimmy was the pleasure they had in being together.

When I became "Mom," I presumed that my definition of "Mom" and Jim's definition of "Mom" were the same, although we did not discuss the specifics of that role. In time, we realized that Jim expected me to have the same relationship with Jimmy that Dixie had

had. I, on the other hand, expected that, along with enjoying Jimmy (he was very cute and enjoyable), I would do things for him that had not been high on the list of priorities with a terminally ill mother in the home. Jim was grateful when I took him for his first visit to a dentist, taught him how to swallow vitamins, limited his intake of cola, and cooked nutritious meals that Jimmy enjoyed eating. Other parental tasks, however, that I considered part of being a good Mom, began to expose the differences in our expectations.

In theory we agreed that he was old enough to learn to clean up his room, make his bed, and share in a few household chores. After he'd learned how to do those chores, and was expected to do them on his own, Jim and I agreed on some reasonable consequences if he refused to do them or didn't do them as instructed. Jim gave me the authority to enforce those rules and consequences when he wasn't home, as a "real" mother would. Whenever Jimmy balked at the increase in his responsibilities, however, Jim would either ease the requirements for successful completion of a job, or would be upset with *me* for administering our agreed upon consequences.

I was caught in the middle, and soon became the "bad guy" in the home. Jimmy did exactly what any kid with any sense would do—he used the division between Jim and me to make life as easy for himself as possible! Who could blame him! The problem wasn't with him, but between Jim and me!

I reacted with increasing outrage because, 1) Jim was punishing me for doing exactly what we had agreed I would do, and 2) what Jimmy was learning best was how to manipulate us. I felt angry with Jim for not seeing what our conflict and inconsistent expectations were doing to Jimmy.   I felt self-righteous and determined to teach Jim how to be a good parent! For *Jimmy's* sake, of course! More and more ours became a house divided. The issue consumed us.

The more extreme Jim and I became, the more I took my anger out on Jimmy, in spite of knowing it wasn't his fault. The more obvious the conflict became, the more the other children took sides. This scenario is not limited to stepfamilies, but, from what we've learned since, it is a classic stepfamily issue . . . the primary one that results in the break-up of many second marriages.

During the same time period my older son, Steven, was getting into trouble. He was disrespectful of boundaries, challenging of any authority, sassing teachers, cutting school, etc. He became unmanageable. I felt helpless and terrified of the road down which I saw him heading.

As a toddler, Steven had been a daddy's boy. He adored his father, and lived for 5:30 p.m. every evening when his Dad's truck would pull into the driveway. He was bright and energetic, and, for a two-year-old firstborn, had a large vocabulary of more than 200 words which was growing daily. When his Dad disappeared from his life without any way for him to understand, he became withdrawn. He lost all but ten or twelve basic words. He reverted to diapers. He wildly panicked every time I left him with anyone but his grandmothers. For several months, whenever he heard the neighbor's pickup truck come down the street, he'd run to the front door yelling, "Daddy! Daddy!" I wanted to die. After more than 30 years, remembering still brings tears to my eyes.

He gradually regained his vocabulary. Eventually he was ready to give up diapers. His body grew, but the propensity to panic remained, along with nightmares and sleepwalking. He exposed his depression by coloring only with black or purple crayons. He was suspicious of anyone he didn't know well. He developed severe allergies and was sick a lot. I became very protective of him. I did not want him hurt by anything, ever again. I was a single parent for thirteen years before marrying Jim.

By 1984 our battle over the "right" way to parent Jimmy was escalating. In addition, I was perpetually teetering on the edge of my resources with Steven's belligerent behavior. One day I was shocked by this awareness: *I was upset with Jim for dealing with Jimmy in exactly the same way as I had dealt with Steven.* Often I had relaxed the rules when he was upset because I felt sorry for him. Jim felt sorry for Jimmy's loss of his mother, and couldn't tolerate his unhappiness for any reason. I had taken more of Steven's shaky security away by allowing him to talk me out of unpleasant consequences. Jimmy was becoming more and more insecure, the longer Jim and I fought. Neither boy had the security that comes from consistent expectations and predictable consequences lovingly enforced.

After several attempts at counseling, Steven would not agree to some very basic house rules, so, when he became 18 years old, he moved out. He was very bitter and I was devastated. In addition, Jim and his daughters, Teri, and Karen, were also angry with me because of my obvious frustration with, and, at times, harsh treatment of Jimmy. Jimmy's tantrums were increasing. Most of my attention was going to the problems with Steven, Jim, and Jimmy. Peter, my other son, felt unimportant and abandoned in the chaos. All of our "happily ever after" dreams had become a marathon nightmare for everyone.

In my perception, I had to choose between saving our marriage or continuing to try to "save" Jimmy. If I continued fighting for what I thought was best for Jimmy, I would lose both Jim and Jimmy. Finally, with the encouragement of our counselor and to Jim's great relief, I relinquished my role as Jimmy's Mom.[63] Jim, in essence, became a single parent again. I turned my attention to changing my own behaviors and attitudes in the battle to save our marriage and my own sanity.

I slowly began to relax my inner and outer criticism of Jim's fathering. After I resigned from my deeply entrenched position of Jimmy's "savior," Jim began to move out of the defensive position of Jimmy's "defender." He began setting and enforcing appropriate, consistent boundaries for Jimmy. Jim consulted with me only on Jimmy-issues that directly affected me. Gradually our marriage began to assume a healthier balance and to heal.

Steven's lifestyle continued to frighten me. His depression and the resultant self-destructive behaviors were out of control. We saw each other frequently, and the love between us never diminished. The overwhelming guilt I felt from what I perceived as my failure to

---

[63] More about this difficult decision in Chapter 13, "For Those Who Are Blending."

rear a healthy, well-adjusted child, however, became a training ground for advanced lessons about co-dependency.[64] For the first few years after he moved out, I was constantly trying to convince him to get help—to "fix" him. I gave him brochures, phone numbers, and leads about one source of help after another. He refused them all. Eventually, I released him to his adulthood, and accepted that whatever I had done or not done, his life was his to live, and the choices he was making were his responsibility alone. He told me that he felt an enormous sense of release when I kindly, but emphatically handed him the full responsibility for his life and quit trying to "save" him.

Meanwhile, my "easy" son, Peter, withheld himself more and more from the family in general, and me in particular. Perhaps he was finally facing all the issues that he had temporarily set aside in favor of survival and getting himself successfully into adulthood. The emotional distance between us was excruciatingly painful for me.

In 1995 I went back to school for a Masters Degree in Spiritual Psychology. As I've stated before, the philosophy embraced in the school was one of personal learning. Everyone was encouraged to "work your process" while earning a degree. The first year's classes laid a strong foundation for me, but in the second year, I dug in for serious personal work.

During one class I was told to choose a relationship where I was experiencing conflict and use the upset feelings to do an exercise called "owning negative projections." I used my hurt and resentfulness toward my son, Peter. I felt unjustly cut off from him. I was frustrated with what I perceived as his refusal to discuss what was wrong! I felt judged as the most horrible mother in the world— and then, in a life altering instant, a buried belief about myself exploded into my conscious awareness. Like film hidden inside a projector was the image, the belief, that I had been a "bad" mother. I was angry with Peter simply because he appeared to be acting in such a way as to validate my own painful belief. At that moment, I "owned," or "recognized," or "assumed responsibility for" my personal judgment that I had failed at the job about which I cared the most. I believed my failure to give him what he needed during his teen years

---

[64] Review codependency in Chapters 8, 9 and 11.

as well as the mistakes I'd made with the other children were inexcusable. I wept.

It seems impossible for me to communicate the enormity of this realization to me. It was easy to see Peter as "wrong" for being so angry with me. It was far more comfortable to see the situation as something *he* needed to change. I felt entirely justified in expecting that he understand that I had done the best I could. I thought he should just grow up . . . or "get over it!" I was knocked flat the moment I realized that (what I perceived as) his rejection of me was excruciatingly painful *because* it mirrored my own *even harsher* rejection of myself as a mother. All of my arguments supporting Peter as the cause of our relationship difficulties lost power. I realized I had far more than he to do with the alienation we were experiencing. That moment of recognition moved the issue from the shadow of my sub-conscious into the light of my awareness where I could begin to do my share of the healing. I was told that healing the issue within *myself* would greatly increase the chances that the issue would eventually be healed in relationship with Peter.

As I continued to follow the directions of the exercise, I realized that my first job was to forgive myself for judging myself as a "bad" mother who didn't deserve forgiveness. I could not expect Peter or Steven, Teri, Karen, or Jimmy to forgive me for the ways they had been hurt by me if I wasn't willing to first forgive myself. I found it impossible to forgive myself instantly, however—the judgment was too deeply believed—so I made the *process* of self-forgiveness one part of my required second-year project. I set up a plan for practicing self-forgiveness.

Before I could even begin to work my plan, however, I discovered I needed to take a preliminary step. I realized that I actually thought I was accomplishing something worthwhile by wallowing in shame and feelings of failure. I believed I could make my family's pain go away if I felt bad enough—that my purgatory would buy healing for them.[65] How foolish and what a waste of energy! Continuing to judge myself as a failure would only keep me stuck in self-pity and a tendency to be over-responsible for their now adult lives. By releasing myself from on-going self-punishment for my

---

[65] A damaging belief if there ever was one!

flawed parenting, I was also releasing them to assume appropriate self-responsibility for working on their own issues with me, just as I had had to work out my issues with my parents.

A more detached perspective helped me begin changing my belief about the worthwhile-ness of clinging to my guilt.[66]   I acknowledged the limited point of view that I have here on earth. How could I set myself up as "judge" and know for *sure* what parts of my parenting had been "bad" and what parts were "good"? Some of the things I had most resented about my parents became the motivating force behind my desire to learn how relationships work. What I learned about relationships had already resulted in the teaching of hundreds of couples in our workshops. Now the writing of this book could possibly help thousands more to enjoy better relationships.   Perhaps there is one measurement of parental performance insofar as an ideal childhood is concerned, and a different measure of performance from a more detached, elevated perspective. Sometimes higher purposes are served by our or others' mistakes or failures.[67]

This is not to excuse or condone anything less than every effort being made to meet every need of every child. This view is offered only as another reason why it makes sense to forgive ourselves of our shortcomings. As adults, each of us has the option of using any circumstance of our lives for our betterment or as an excuse for bitterness.

As I began to accept that continuing to feel bad about myself as a mother would not help any of us one little bit, I gathered the courage to tackle the work of self-forgiveness. In spite my belief that self-forgiveness was the only sane course of action, the shame and self-judgment were too deeply entrenched to let go of easily. The job required dedication to a long-term process. Every morning while I walked, with my hand over my heart, I repeated this litany: "I forgive myself for judging myself as a bad mother. The truth is, every day of my motherhood, I have done the very best I knew how to do at that time." In addition, any other time I was aware of feeling "bad" or

---

[66] See Chapter 6 about how to change a belief.
[67] James Hillman in <u>The Soul's Code: In Search of Character and Calling</u>, examined what the circumstances of our lives may mean in terms of our true destiny. (1996) New York: Random House.

judging myself as a "bad" mother, I would repeat the words, trying to let them sink into my wounded heart. Months passed without much progress. The feelings of shame and self-judgment continued to surface frequently. It felt as if I were trying to break up a huge granite boulder with an ice pick!

The full story of my journey of self-forgiveness will, perhaps, be told another time. It's enough to say that after several months, I experienced a major breakthrough with a significant reduction in the amount of judgment I held against myself. I began to really receive my own forgiveness deep within my being. Since that time, I occasionally have to repeat the refrain, but, for the most part, I am free of the unbearable weight of judging myself as a "bad" mother.

I am grateful that Peter, also, was "doing his work." Over time we have both worked at healing our relationship. I treasure his love and admire the wonderful man that he is.

While I was in the process of forgiving myself, I realized even more profoundly than I had before that I had projected my judgments of myself as a parent onto Jim. It was easier to judge Jim for being a "bad" parent than to look at the same ways I had parented Steven. By criticizing the "speck" in Jim's eye I had avoided looking at the "board"[68] in my own.   As I forgave myself, I began forgiving Jim for what I perceived as his faults as a parent. The more my compassion grew for my own imperfections, the more compassion I had for him. The more compassion I had for us, the more understanding and forgiving I became of my own parents. They, too, had done the very best that they knew how to do as parents. And as I released us all from harsh judgment, my compassion grew to include all parents, everywhere. What an enormous, overwhelming responsibility it is to bring another life into the world and try to prepare him or her for adulthood. All of us come to the job with no experience and, to one degree or another, flawed tools. None of us is perfect. All of us do the best we know how to do.

---

[68] Jesus talked about the concept of projections with this metaphor. He is quoted in Matthew 7:3,4 and Luke 6:41,42, The Living Bible.

Years have gone by since our family was in such chaos. Each member of the family, in individual ways and at different paces, began to forgive. Jimmy still calls me "Mom" and I love him dearly. With amazing grace, he honors me with his respect and affection. Teri and Karen generously began to see that there were two sides to the issue and have both worked very hard in the process of healing their relationships with me. Peter had to assume a great deal of self-responsibility in order to move forward into adulthood. He has invested lot of effort into healing the wounds he suffered during that crazy time. It is my joy to be warmly welcomed into the circle of his life and family. Steven has moved through his own unique process of acceptance and forgiveness. Gradually we began to feel like a family whose members were glad to be a family rather than a group of individuals who were locked in a desperate arrangement together.

These few pages chronicle in part, the biggest projection I have ever had to "own" and work to clear. The same process, however, proved true (although didn't take as long to complete) when I tried it with the annoying cashier at the car wash who expected me to go find the workers to wash my car. She didn't want to care for me as a customer. (I, too, am lax about taking care of my own needs, at times.) It held true when I was upset with Steven for remaining stuck in some self-defeating behaviors. (I am stuck with some behaviors that I'm not ready to change, as well.) And so on, and so on. Every time I experience an upsetting internal reaction toward another, I can track those upset feelings back to a quality or behavior in myself that I judge as "bad".

In that way, my relationship with others often reflects my inner relationship with myself. Owning (taking appropriate responsibility for) and clearing a projection is an act of liberation, the taking back of power. The process takes energy that is being drained away by negative, destructive emotions and directs that energy to healing and loving. It also brings compassion and forgiveness to myself *and* the person or event that triggered the upset. Clearing the projection does not mean that I must accept the situation as it is, or helplessly submit to disrespectful treatment of me. It is simply a foundational first step that clears my inner air of anger and judgment so that I am able to take non-judgmental, neutral, and appropriately self-responsible steps of action. Owning and clearing my projections help me claim the full measure of my power for governing my own life, rather than manipulating others.

For instance, I may "own" the projection of resenting the abusive way a particular person yells at me. My resentment is exposing the dislike I have for my tendency to *abuse myself* with excessive sugar, or lack of sleep, for instance. In clearing the projection, I forgive them, forgive myself, and then with healthier internal balance, set a self-honoring boundary with appropriate consequences to stop that abusive behavior. In this case I said to the person who was yelling at me over the phone, "I want to keep talking with you, but if you continue to yell at me, I'm going to hang up." He kept yelling so I quietly hung up the phone...*without anger.*

Another example might be an adult child living at home who refuses to accept responsibilities appropriate for shared living space. I may "own" the projection of impatience and irritation with him or her, knowing that I, also, choose to act irresponsibly at times; and, after forgiving myself and the child, release the anger and judgments. With my inner air cleared, I may now, from a place of respect and love, decide to say, "Loving you unconditionally does not mean I must tolerate your behavior unconditionally. If you do not agree to and comply with the responsibilities I'm asking of you within the next two weeks, you may not live here."[69]

What upsets are you experiencing in your life? Do you have a relationship that is rocky? Are you courageous enough to see if those upset feelings might be originating from an image in your "projector"?

At the end of this chapter is a suggested format for exploring upsets. Doing the work of recognizing and owning your projections

---

[69] There are several great books that include explanations of the setting and enforcing of reasonable, age-appropriate boundaries. They are listed in the bibliography at the end of this volume.

onto your spouse, your child, or any other individual, is perhaps, the hardest inner self-work in the world. It is also the most liberating. Take a chance. Be brave. Do the following exercise using the most upsetting issue you can think of that mars your relationship with someone you love. I dare you!

Puzzle Piece #9: I am courageously facing the issues within myselfthat create or contribute to the issues in my marriage.

"Outer experience is a reflection of inner reality."
Mary Hulnick[70]

"Why worry about a speck in the eye of a brother
when you have a board in your own? . . .
First get rid of the board.
Then you can see to help your brother."
Matthew 7:3,5

---

[70] Hulnick, Mary, Ph.D., Vice President, University of Santa Monica, Santa Monica, CA.

Identifying and Clearing a Negative Projection

Do *not* try to do this exercise in your head. Projections tend to be slippery. The subconscious mind sometimes works overtime to avoid the momentary pain of acknowledging self-judgments. So, on your computer, or with a pad and pen, write out the answers with as much detail as comes to mind in order to derive the greatest benefit from the exercise.

1. What happened that triggered this upset and how do I feel?
   (This is the appropriate place to thoroughly vent the feelings. See Book #1, Chapter 12.)
   For instance: "I feel so angry!" or "I feel hurt," or "I feel frightened," etc.

2. Answer any questions that seem to fit your situation:
   - What am I thinking about this? What is my opinion?
   - What do I believe about why this happened or how he/she/they should have acted?
   - Is there something I expect or need from this person that I didn't get or am not getting?
   - Is my *real* expectation or need something that this person can't reasonably be expected to give me? When I expect another person to make my pain go away, or make me feel whole, or read my mind, or prove that I'm lovable, desirable, successful, or make my life perfect, or (fill in the blank) I am doomed to disappointment. Some needs cannot be met by another. If that is what I deep-down expect, I have an irrational belief.
   - What is (are) my judgment(s)? (Tip: If there's an upset, there *is* a judgment! Name it!)
     For instance: "I believe she is rude in the way she treated me."
     "The way they are doing it is wrong. They should know better."
     "How could she do this to me? A real friend wouldn't act this way!"
     "He's a terrible person! A loser!"
     "A loving God wouldn't let this happen!"
     "It's only right that he be the one to change. After all, he's at fault!"
     "She should know better and be the first to apologize."

Notice that all of these irrational beliefs or opinions are focused on persons or events over which I have no control and, perhaps, have limited understanding. The subject of irrational beliefs is explored more thoroughly in Chapter 6.

3. What are my choices?
   For instance: I can remain upset, blaming another for my pain, or I can use this situation as an opportunity to learn more about myself, exercise self-responsibility, and empower personal growth. If I'm willing to look at the possible projection, an appropriate intention could be, "I will take my power back by resolving this inner upset and find a healthy way to resolve the outer conflict."

4. As I review the answers to the questions listed under #2, can any of those opinions, beliefs, or judgments be applied to some aspect of myself? Do I do essentially the same thing in a different arena? Are there ways that I demonstrate the same quality toward myself or another? Do I self-righteously believe that I am not capable of acting the same way if driven by extreme circumstances? This step requires brutal honesty and a willingness to clearly examine myself. Remember the suggested intention—to clarify my next step and to heal, not to judge, beat up, or shame myself. Accepting something unpleasant as true about myself doesn't mean I am resigned to stay that way.

5. Am I willing to extend compassion and forgiveness to myself, first, and then to any others involved?
   For instance: I have found it helpful to put my hand over my heart and say "I forgive myself for judging myself as ___________. The truth is, I was doing the best I knew how to do at that time and I am willing to use this experience to help me remember to do better in the future." Or, "I forgive myself for judging (name of other person) as ___________. (Name) is doing the best he or she can."

6. How do I feel now? If I feel a sense of relief, some or all of the projection has been cleared and I'm ready to move on to step seven, if needed. If I feel better but still somewhat upset, I may need to do this exercise regularly until the *process* of forgiveness[71]

is complete. Until then, if possible, I'll wait until the next steps are clear, or I'll do the best I can with how far I've come so far.

7. What beliefs will I choose to replace the irrational beliefs? If I believed _________ instead, would this new belief help me remain balanced with this person or circumstance? Would this belief be more self-honoring? Would this belief help me choose appropriate boundaries?

> For instance, what if I truly believe that the other person is doing the best that he or she knows how to do? What if I believe that that person is in my life for the purpose of helping me grow? (To help me learn to me more assertive, perhaps, or to force me to value my needs enough to stand up for them…) What if my challenge with this person is exactly what is needed to motivate me to move forward in my own life? What if this person is a messenger to assist me in giving up an attitude of victim-hood and strengthening my ability to be self-honoring? What if the healing of this issue within me is exactly what is needed before I can go on to experience what I really want for my life?

8. How can I apply this learning in my relationship with this person? What outer steps do I need to take?
   a. Did I behave in such a way that it would be appropriate for me to apologize?
      Often when I am upset, I treat the other person disrespectfully. It is a self-honoring choice to apologize for my behavior, even if the other person does not accept responsibility for his or her role in the event. I do this to be in alignment with my own integrity as much as for the other person. Other times, the upset has been within oneself, and apologizing to the object of our upset would open an unnecessary "can of worms".
   b. Is there some way my behavior or role needs to be adjusted in this relationship?
      If the upset is over a lack of appreciation for what I do, perhaps I need to do less in order to stay in balance. Perhaps I need to

---

[71] It may help to review parts of Chapter 7, "Do I Have To?"

honor myself with more free time, or nurturing experiences. If the relationship is toxic, and the other person is not willing to refrain from abusive or disrespectful behavior, perhaps it is necessary to limit or eliminate contact with that person. If my children are out-of-control and I am frequently yelling, perhaps I need to make some changes in my methods of parenting. Perhaps a parenting class where I can share and get feedback or seeing a parenting coach would be helpful.

c. Is there something I can do to help myself remain balanced so that I can make choices from a more centered, evaluative place in the future?   With one relationship in my life in which remaining balanced was a problem, I arranged to only see this person when another person was with me, never when I was alone. In other instances, it was very liberating for me to realize that I didn't have to make decisions immediately. When I allowed myself to take an hour or a day before responding to a request, I was giving myself the time to reach a balanced decision. For a long time my standard answer to any request was, "May I get back to you with an answer tomorrow?" Without this practice I tended to make impulsive decisions that I later regretted, and tended to blame the other person.

d. Would it be appropriate to ask for a mirroring date with this person, respectfully sharing my feelings or needs so that a mutually agreeable adjustment may be made? Do I need to establish some appropriate boundary with consequences if it is violated?

9. I acknowledge and appreciate myself for my willingness to identify and clear my projection!

Owning projections is an Advanced Course in Self-Responsibility and is deserving of self-acknowledgment for the willingness to tackle it. If you've gained new insight and taken a step forward toward appropriate self-responsibility while completing this exercise, treat yourself to a pat on the back, tickets to a favorite sport, a hug from a friend, or bubble-bath! You've earned a reward!

**"An attitude of judgment doesn't break (humble) me;
it puffs me up. It fills me with arrogance.**

**When I learn to give respect, I become transformed in
the process."72
Gary Thomas**

*"Don't fool yourself into thinking that you are really
working on your marriage
if that little inner voice is shouting,
'S/he's wrong, let him/her change first.'
You are only wasting time.
You first need to rid yourself of that distraction before
you can do anything constructive about your marriage."
Michele Weiner Davis73*

---

72 Thomas, Gary, (2000). <u>Sacred Marriage,</u> p. 62. Grand Rapids, MI: Zondervan
73 Davis, Michele Weiner, (2001). <u>The Divorce Remedy,</u> p. 149. New York: Simon
& Schuster.

Chapter 11

Real Life Recovery

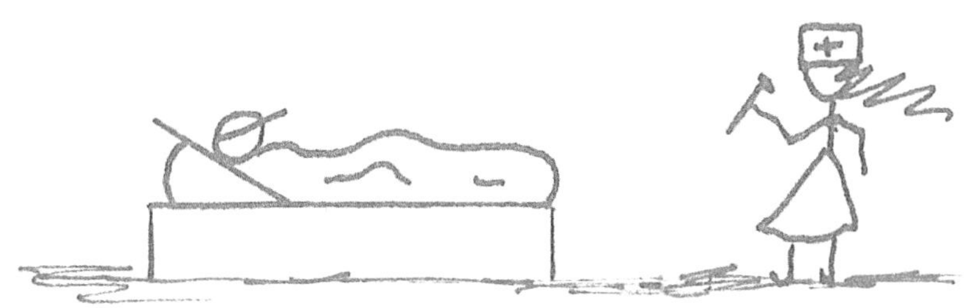

Therapist: "What kinds of feelings have you been experiencing this week?"
Wife: "I've been feeling confused and depressed."
Husband: "No you haven't!"

A great deal of my motivation for self-examination and learning new ways to relate came because the persons close to me wouldn't change! The rest of it came from my unhappiness with the way *I* was behaving. Bit by bit I became willing to explore ways that *I* could change that might be more effective in meeting my own needs and the healthy needs of the relationship. Every time I assumed responsibility for my own needs and my own role in a particular relationship, I was turning from entangled co-dependency to a real relationship, as well as from martyrdom to self-respect. It was a happy coincidence (that I now know to be a law on which I can count) that in each instance, I was also treating my loved one with more respect.

By the time he was 17, Steve had purchased three old wrecks of Camaros and pieced together one sometimes-working car. One of the Camaro skeletons was left in our backyard. Weeds were growing up through the floorboards, just as I'd expect to see in a junkyard, but not on my property! I was embarrassed. For months I had been asking him to dispose of it. He kept promising me he would. Deadlines came and went without any action being taken. Does this sound familiar? It's much harder to be tough with a beloved son than a carpenter! (Chapter 8, Velcro.) Finally, recognizing the similarity to the sewing room saga, I asked Steve when he thought he could reasonably get the Camaro carcass out of the yard. He gave me a date about two weeks away. I told him that I was sure he would take care of it, but if the car was still there at 3 p.m. on the day he'd given me, I'd call a wrecker to come and get it. He said, "Sure." I quit nagging.

The day before the deadline I quietly reminded him of his agreement and my promise. He acted blasé. The following day, he came to me about noon with his list of "good" reasons why he hadn't been able to move the car. I listened, then quietly told him I was sorry but I'd be calling the wrecker at 3 p.m. He was shocked. He got quite angry. Before, it had always been me who was angry, while he was "cool." I discovered that the one in control doesn't have to be angry. Before, he'd been in control of me *and* the yard. Now I was.

I think it's important at this point to say that I was *not* in control of Steven. He was free to move the car himself or allow it to be moved by the wrecker. That was his choice. But he was no longer in control of making our property into a junkyard! And he was not in control of me. The property was mine (ours). I had the legal and ethical right to make decisions concerning the property based on what I liked or didn't like. I had abdicated that right to Steven by giving him the freedom to break his agreements with me. I simply resumed control of my right to choose in matters concerning myself or my property. Then he could choose what he wanted to do or not do in response.

He stomped around and yelled for about ten minutes, then left. As is often the case, separating the Velcro strips of our co-dependent relationship was noisy! An hour later he was back with a buddy and his trailer. They loaded the car and hauled it to a storage yard where Steve had to pay for the privilege of storing it. My backyard was clean.

When things quieted down, we talked. I admitted that I had trained him to expect that I wouldn't follow through with my word. (This is a classic case of projection—my being unhappy with *him* for something *I* was doing!) I had taught him that he could count on me to back down from any painful consequences. He told me that he'd learned that if he could just survive the lecture, then he could expect to be rescued.

Steven continued to be my most valuable resource in "recovering" from co-dependent behavior. He consistently exposed layer after layer of mixed motives, faulty beliefs, and dysfunctional, irrational needs in me. Thanks to his faithful "teaching," after a lot of noise, and even more pain, I eventually learned to set reasonable boundaries to keep myself from playing the role of a victim. I learned how to make decisions honoring *myself* that also honored him—his ability to make his own choices and experience the consequences, pleasant or not, from those choices. After many years of struggling with the sticky Velcro of our relationship, Steve and I both broke free, allowing us the hard won, sweet pleasure of just loving each other without hidden agendas.

Recovery from co-dependency is *never* about controlling another person. The other half of a Velcro relationship will simply do whatever he or she will do. Given what he or she does, recovery is totally about assuming *appropriate* responsibility for myself, my welfare, my needs, or decisions which can only, with good mental health, be made by me.

In addition, it's important to clarify that recovery from co-dependency is *not* about each person being totally and independently responsible only for him or herself. One of the most valuable assets of being in partnership is known as "selectivity"—that is the dividing of chores according to who does what best. Jim has assumed the responsibility of "primary bread-winner." He is usually the one who takes the trash cans out to the street on trash pick-up day, does most of the negotiations when we refinance the house or buy insurance, and is *always* the one who kills any spiders. I have assumed the primary responsibility for our bookkeeping, shopping, decorating, arranging family gatherings, and preparing for our workshops or speaking engagements. Jobs that we both dislike are divided between us or we trade back and forth. Division of labor is efficient. It makes sense. It makes the "partnership" run more smoothly.

What makes "selectivity" work is that responsibilities are equally shared. The equal sharing keeps this scenario from being co-dependent. There are days that I do lazy things while Jim is officiating for five weddings! There are evenings when he's watching a baseball game while I'm writing or coaching a distressed couple! But overall, we contribute an equal amount of energy to the successful running of our little partnership.

Things that create the wall of resentment in a relationship are defined by the term, "co-dependency." The best definition of co-dependency that I've ever heard is "an imbalance of responsibility." The following paragraphs are little vignettes that have occurred in our relationship or have been shared by couples in my office or in our workshops. In each vignette an imbalance of responsibility is adding one or more blocks to the wall that separates loved ones, making a healthy SoulMate relationship impossible.

In the car: "Your driving is unsafe! I am a nervous wreck every time I have to ride with you. Did you read about the accident in the paper that happened because the driver was doing what you're doing? You need a traffic safety course."

Recovery: Apologize for the nagging and insults. Ask for a mirroring session where you can express your feelings respectfully and take several minutes to plan the words you will use. If you have co-operation, brainstorm a driving agreement. Jim and I agree that the driver slows down or leaves more space between cars whenever the passenger requests it. The driving conditions always seem more dangerous from the passenger seat because the passenger is out of control! Jim also agreed to move to the right lane of the freeway at least one mile before the desired exit. One wife asks to be let out to take a cab when her husband is reckless. For another couple, the wife always drives because she is so afraid of his driving. Do whatever works for the two of you without creating resentment.

In this example, recovery is when the uncomfortable one takes full responsibility for his/her feelings and first tries to work out a solution agreeable to both partners. If that doesn't work, then find a solution that takes care of your need to feel safe, allowing your partner to feel whatever feelings come up as a result of your *respectful* decision.

Scene: "He never turns his underwear or socks right side out before putting them in the laundry! I resent the extra work!"

Recovery: Leave them inside out. They wash just as clean that way. If it's important to him, he can turn them right side out before dressing.

Scene: "I resent the way you've let yourself go. I wish you would take better care of yourself. I don't like the extra weight you are carrying. I am embarrassed to be seen with you."

Recovery: Do the Owning Negative Projections exercise, Chapter 10. Make a list of ways I used to treat my partner as special that I am no longer doing. Apologize for the hurtful comments and judgments. Plan a mirroring session where just my feelings will be spoken, not my judgments. I hope that those feelings will be concern for your partner's health. Ask if there are specific ways that I can be more supportive or if there are outside sources of help I can encourage my partner to pursue.   It is not appropriate to expect my partner to boost my own sense of worth by the way he or she appears. My partner is not an object to bolster my flagging self-worth, but a human being who deserves to be accepted and loved. Bottom line, I cannot force my partner to live healthily. I can only be responsible for my own health and body condition, and for the quality of unconditional love I give. Jim and I agreed not to monitor each other's eating habits. We are not each other's watch-dog. (Neither of us ever said anything as crass as the scene described here, although I've coached couples where such things have been said.)

Scene: "I resent the way he forgets special occasions. He never remembers my birthday or his mother on Mother's Day. He bought me a toaster for Christmas! I feel angry when I have to remind him of special occasions. If he loved me he would be more aware of these things."

Recovery: What he does or doesn't do with his mother on Mother's Day is none of my business. That is between him and his mother. If I choose to, I send her a card representative of *my* relationship with her. I will not measure love based on whether or not my gift expectations have been met. I will, however, ask for a mirroring date to share my feelings respectfully about this issue and then brainstorm some practical solutions such as:

1. Give him a list of stores from which I would welcome gift certificates.
2. Ask if I can make a shopping date with him when an occasion approaches.
3. Agree on an amount of money I can spend on myself for special occasions.
4. Ask if it's O.K. for me to write a reminder in his date book with suggestions of things I would like.
5. Initiate a discussion of love languages. Tell him my feelings when I am remembered with a gift.
6. Determine to positively reinforce with gratitude every remembrance or expression of love that is offered.

Scene: "She is so bossy. She is constantly telling me what to do. I feel like a little boy being harassed by his mother. She is so afraid I won't complete a project that she nags me about it. In reaction, I procrastinate even more to punish her."

Recovery: It again begins with a mirroring session where my feelings can be respectfully shared. I open it by confessing my tactic of deliberate procrastination and apologize for practicing that underhanded method of communication. When we each have been heard we brainstorm some solutions along the line of:

1. Wife agrees to ask once and then drop it unless choosing to bring up the issue respectfully again in a mirroring session.
2. Husband agrees to give a reasonable date by which project will be completed. He is accountable to keep his word.
3. If unforeseen events require postponement, he talks about them with his wife, and sets a new date for which he is responsible.
4. If several postponements occur, husband acknowledges his responsibility for the consequence of undermining her trust in his word and accepts responsibility for the time and effort it will take to regain her trust. Back to mirroring.
5. If necessary, agree on a date beyond which the wife will step in to do the project without interference, or someone will be hired to complete it without *any* complaint by the husband.

Scene: "She never balances the checkbook! She won't stick to a budget! The bills aren't paid on time and our credit rating is being damaged. We were turned down for a lower interest mortgage because of our poor credit rating. I resent being the victim of her financial irresponsibility!"

Recovery: This might be tricky. For some reason, most of us are so vulnerable when it comes to money issues. The solution must begin with a mirroring session or perhaps many of them. It might be helpful to explore what money means to each of us. What do I need from a perfect credit rating besides a lower interest loan? What does money or the relaxed attitude toward money do for my wife? Why is it such an emotionally threatening issue? How can we negotiate a way of handling our finances that meets both of our needs? Possible solutions if agreed upon by both:

1. Use an envelope method of paying for household expenses. Each pay period a set amount of cash goes into the grocery envelope, the clothing envelope, the gas envelope, etc. It's gone when it's gone.
2. A date is set for paying bills together, or one person pays them and gives a report to the other so both know where the account stands.
3. The husband must agree not to nag or insult, and the wife would consent to stay within the agreed-upon limits. Both understand that keeping their agreements is the foundation of SoulMate trust. Terms can be renegotiated if either feels the need.
4. Jim and I have found that we each need an "allowance," money for which we don't have to answer to each other. We also set aside a "couple allowance" every week—money with which we do things together. During our worst financial time, the personal weekly allowance was $5 each and the couple (date) allowance was $20. As our financial condition has become better, our allowances have become more generous.
5. If these options don't work, do what you would do if you wanted to learn how to dance or do wood-working . . . take lessons! Interview several financial planners describing what you need. Ask how he or she might support you in learning. Hire the one with whom you are the most comfortable. Or take an adult education class together.

Advanced recovery from codependency is learning to apply the concepts to feelings as well as behaviors. Each person is not only responsible for the *behaviors* chosen but the *feelings* felt or, at the least, how the feelings are managed. One of my greatest challenges as a relationship coach is to weed out "she/he makes me feel" from a person's speech pattern. As a culture we seem to support the notion that another person is responsible for how I feel—therefore, my feelings are that person's fault. In addition, one national pass-time is trying to guess what another person is thinking or feeling so an appropriate response can be planned. I confess I frequently catch myself at this fruitless game, even yet.

Inner thought: "He said he's glad to take me to the doctor and be with me during this painful test, but I don't know if he really means it. What if he really doesn't want to go and will be resentful about being there? I think I'll just drive myself to make sure. But I'm frightened of the test and want him to be with me. I wish he would express himself more *emphatically* so I could be sure he meant it."

Recovery: None of us can read another person's mind. Each person is responsible to speak his or her own truth. I am responsible to tell my partner that I want his support while going through the test. My partner is responsible to tell the truth about whether or not he wants to be there or can be there. I must assume my partner is telling the truth. I act on what I've been told. I do not hold myself responsible for guessing what is true for my partner. If what is said is not true, he or she must deal with the consequence of that deceit. In the future my partner will perhaps learn to be more careful about speaking the truth.

A natural consequence of not speaking the truth is being present at events about which I don't care, or even resent attending. Jim and I have an agreement to always tell the truth about such events. If I want to see a certain movie but Jim doesn't, I go alone or with a friend. If he is invited to sing at an event I'd rather skip, I skip it. We use a value scale to help us decide about exceptions to this agreement. For example, the event is one I must attend. If I feel particularly vulnerable or I'm going to receive a meaningful award, I'll say to Jim, "On a scale of one to ten, the importance to me that you are with me is an eight." If the importance to me is above a six, Jim invariably chooses to go with me as a love gift to me, even if he would, otherwise, choose not to attend. Both of us are responsible to use this scale truthfully. If used indiscriminately to get the other one to do things of lessor importance, it would lose its meaning.

It is impossible to over-emphasize the importance of each person being responsible to tell the truth—respectfully and as kindly as possible, but the truth. Healthy relationships, especially of SoulMate quality, can only be built on the truth.

Scene: "My spouse is an addict."

Recovery: The following story is about Dan and Angie and their struggle with Dan's addiction.   Although his particular addiction is to cocaine, all addictions (spending, eating disorders, sex, rage, drugs, alcohol, work) have the same root causes and require the same process of healing.   Ones in close relationship with an addict are often drawn into the bottomless pit of codependency.

When they married ten years before, Angie was unaware that Dan struggled with a cocaine addiction. It was not a daily, or even weekly occurrence, but every few months Dan would disappear for three to five days at a time on a cocaine binge. Angie soon became familiar with the routine: the anguish of not knowing if he was alive or dead; the fear of how much money would disappear this time, or how much debt there would be to repay; the loneliness of waiting; the shame of finding herself married to a drug addict, a role she never, in her wildest imagination, thought would be true of her; the rage when he returned home looking like a derelict; the fruitless attempts to protect their assets; the exhausting process of "cleaning up the mess" after each binge; the fear of others finding out that led to lies to their families, employers, and friends; the dashed hopes after one recovery attempt after another; the desolation of her failure to be enough to motivate Dan to kick his habit; her terror that others would judge her as stupid for staying with him.

When clean, Dan was extremely intelligent, thoughtful, repentant, a good provider, a man with a good heart—someone she would choose, again, with whom to spend the rest of her life. She believes that if he was a jerk, or beat her, or wasn't sorry, or was uncouth in his habits, or brought his drug-life home with him, it would have been easy for her to leave. But during his clean periods, which sometimes lasted up to two years, Angie's love for him was renewed, and she hoped, again, that this time it would last.

Over the years, Angie learned of her role in the addiction dynamic from family counseling during drug rehabs, attendance at Codependents Anonymous (a national support network for the families of substance abusers listed in your local phone book), and personal counseling. She gradually became willing to face the fears that kept her imprisoned by Dan's choices. She became less willing to clean up the post-binge messes for him, worked at becoming more financially independent, and increasingly was more supportive of her own right to plan a life for herself that included the stability she craved. As much as she loved Dan, she courageously examined whether she wanted to gamble on him with her life and the lives of the children she wanted to have.

In practical terms, these inner changes took the form of working hard to take care of herself when he was "out." She made an effort to eat, where before she'd be so distraught she couldn't. She focused on trusting a loving God with her uncertain future, rather than holding Dan solely responsible for giving her what she wanted. She gathered the courage to tell her family what they were battling, rather than cutting herself off from their emotional support. She continued advancing at her job, earning enough raises to reassure herself that, if necessary, she could support herself. She quit lying to cover for Dan, and realized that a lot of the motivation behind the lying was the attempt to protect herself, not him, from others' judgments. She loosened her control on the family finances, realizing that being the sole keeper of the money did not prevent a determined addict from finding a way to get it, and acknowledging that the policy had discouraged Dan from assuming appropriate adult responsibilities. When Dan returned from "going out" she, for the most part, refrained from venting her anger on him, realizing that shaming him with her rage didn't accomplish anything positive, and expressed more compassion for his struggle.

As her self-esteem grew, she gathered the strength to confront her father about some long-festering issues in their relationship. When her parents reacted to the news of Dan's addiction with rage toward Dan and dictatorial advice for her, she told them what she needed was their belief in her ability to find her way through this challenge. More and more, Angie became responsible for her life, rather than playing the role of a victim.

In the meantime, Dan was working hard, as well. The "going out" times grew further and further apart. He very successfully completed post-graduate work with honors and moved into a more challenging and rewarding career. He saw a counselor regularly, discovered that acupuncture treatments helped diminish the physical part of the addiction, worked at stabilizing his routines, and examined the deep hungers that fueled the need for an altered reality. He realized he had assumed the role of scapegoat in his family of origin and began to see that he could choose a different role for himself. He slowly began to believe that although he had done many things for which he felt regret, he deserved to be treated with respect. He refused, however, to acknowledge that some of his distorted beliefs could lead only to the despair that occasionally overwhelmed him and led to drug use. He would not assume responsibility for exchanging those beliefs for ones that would support a healthier lifestyle. He resisted admitting his dependence on a Higher Power and avoided developing inter-dependent, healthy relationships with others in recovery. He thought he could stay clean by simply exerting more control over himself.

A few months after their tenth anniversary and eight months after his last episode, Dan "went out" again for four days. This time Angie ate and slept better than before, almost continuously released Dan into God's loving care, and trusted that her life, as well, was in God's hands. When Dan returned, she lovingly told him she was glad he was home safe. She calmly told him, however, that she would stay in a motel for the next three nights because she would not put herself through the torture of watching while his body tried to heal from the devastation of the cocaine binge. She spent those three nights alone, got a massage, went to see some movies, prayed a lot, and discovered that she could survive without Dan.

A few days later they met in my office. When asked to decide what her bottom-line was in regard to her marriage to Dan, she courageously rose to the challenge.

With kindness, compassion, and extraordinary clarity she delivered this message to Dan: "I love you. I will always love you. I feel compassion for your struggle with cocaine. But I deserve to have the life I want. I want a home of my own and children with a man I can depend on to be there. You have until the end of this year (about ten months) to demonstrate that you are doing everything within your power to permanently kick this addiction and help me build the life I want. That means doing whatever recovery work you've been unwilling to do in the past and saving enough money so that we can buy a house next year and plan for a child. If, at the end of this year, I can't see enough progress then I will leave you. I am still young enough to find someone who will help me build a stable life and have a family."

The words were ones of tender compassion delivered hand in hand with clear boundaries. Angie spoke them with the power of her conviction that she deserved what she wanted from life and they rang with the sound of freedom—freedom from bitterness and victim-hood. I wanted to stand and cheer!

Dan heard Angie's bottom line. He loves her and wants her to have the life she deserves. He deeply desires that life to be with him. He had not come to the meeting empty-handed. He had already begun taking the steps he previously resisted and has, since, faithfully attended a highly successful, local recovery program. He is making friends, exchanging phone numbers, and sharing honestly in the group. He is determined to be a man of integrity in *all* areas of his life. He is admitting his dependence on God for help and gathering hope from those further along in recovery. He is treating himself with more kindness than in the past, rather than self-hatred. He is fighting hard to believe that he, as well as Angie, can have a fulfilling, happy, well-balanced life that is permanently free from the chaos of drug addiction.

Although, at this writing, the final chapters of this story have not been lived, I include it as a profound example of recovery from the dysfunction of codependency and, in this case, recovery from the disease of addiction, as well. Love, compassion, and strong boundaries *can* be delivered simultaneously.

In our workshops, I've been surprised by the resistance to the idea of making contracts. Marriage *is* a contract! A successful marriage requires the ultimate in accountability and trustworthiness. Why are we surprised when many mini-contracts are needed in order to make the primary contract work? This is especially true when each partner is committed to personal growth and determined to weed out the personal irresponsibilities that erect a barrier to a SoulMate relationship. Any behavior modification therapist will emphasize the enormous value of being accountable to someone while in the process of changing an unwanted behavior.

I believe that the resistance comes from an irrational belief that a marriage *should* be successful because of romantic love alone, but nothing kills romantic love faster than the loss of trust that is the consequence of a broken agreement.

When Jim and I became aware of how devastating and divisive resentment was to our relationship, we made this contract: We will only do things for one another that can be done gladly. If I know I will feel resentful while doing something for Jim, I will not agree to do it. Sometimes I initially feel resentful, but if I remember things Jim has done for me, I can negotiate within myself until I am willing, if not glad, to do the requested favor. If, after thought, I know I would still feel resentful, I say, "no."

The benefit of this "contract" is that when Jim is doing me a favor, I know it's because he freely chooses to do it, which makes it easy for me to receive with gratitude. If he says, "no" then I pursue other options without resentment because I don't want the emotional blocks of resentment that would separate our SoulMate intimacy.

I notice that I've used the word "liberated" several times to describe my feeling after a co-dependent bond was broken. Changing co-dependent patterns isn't easy, but both Jim and I have experienced the most exhilarating sense of liberation following each step of recovery, as though we'd been let out of prison.

You may also have noticed that "apology" is included in the recovery sections fairly often. The foundation of responsibility is accepting that our choices have consequences to ourselves and to others. Like appreciation, the words of an apology are simple to give. The words must be heart-felt, however, or they do more damage than good. After some practice, sincerely saying, "I'm sorry," "I was wrong," and "Will you forgive me?" becomes easier. Those words are an essential part of building a SoulMate relationship. None of us comes to marriage as a perfect spouse. Each of us makes mistakes or has some rough edges that cause pain. A SoulMate says, "I'm sorry."

An apology is a great start, but the next essential step is a change of behavior and attitude that proves your good intentions. The keeping of the "contracts" (or agreements if you prefer) is the only means within my power to restore my spouse's trust in me. Trust is built by *behavior*, not words, and one of the most precious qualities of a SoulMate relationship is mutual trust.

Creating a SoulMate relationship won't happen overnight or when you reach the end of this book. Jim and I believe this book is a relationship primer. We hope it will be used as a textbook for building or re-building a successful SoulMate relationship. There are several authors who have done a thorough job of describing anger management, or successful communication, or co-dependency, or belief changes. (Some are listed in the bibliography of this book). In this book I not only provide an overview of all of these issues, but I also offer real-life examples of how we made these changes. Each couple will respond in a unique way, but sometimes it helps to see the way someone else handled a situation.

One couple has attended three of our workshops. (Bless their hearts!) They've told us that each time they have come they hear something that they weren't ready to work on before but are now ready to tackle. Reading this book might be a little like that. You may read some chapters and know you're not ready to tackle that aspect of your relationship. Then you read another chapter and know that you can work on improving *that* part of your relationship.

We were surprised (and so were many of the couples with whom we've worked) how quickly the wall of blame and resentment came down once we were fully committed to doing the work. Your partner may not be as excited about this project as you are at this moment. Do *your* work. Keep your attention focused on your own responsibility. It won't take long for your partner to notice the change. A marriage (or any relationship) is a closed system. That means that when I change something about me, it will automatically change the relationship.

Just as the blocks were added to the wall one by one, they can be removed one by one. The most important tool for breaking down the wall is simply my willingness to assume responsibility for my experience in this relationship. That willingness will make it possible for me to learn new, healthier ways of participating in this relationship one concept at a time, one issue at a time.

These are questions I ask myself to help me identify whether or not I'm in danger of participating in a Velcro relationship, or to clarify healthy boundaries:

When I feel resentful . . .
- Have I assumed a responsibility that isn't rightfully mine? Who's problem is it?
- Have I assumed more responsibility than is my fair share?
- Am I trying to "save" a loved one from experiencing the consequences of his or her choices?
- Have I agreed to contribute more of myself (energy, time, or emotions) than I can gladly give?
- Am I helping or giving to someone else to the detriment or neglect of my own needs?
- Do I want the other person to change his or her behavior so I won't have to change mine?
- (In my experience this last question is frequently the biggy!)

When someone is angry with me . . .
- Do I expect this person to "understand" my irresponsibility?
- Have I expected this person to fulfill my responsibility for me?
- Have I demanded or accepted that this person suffer consequences that are rightfully mine?
- Do I expect this person to "fix" a situation for me or provide a solution?

    (The first four questions might be answered "yes" when I am trying to get away with irresponsibility.)
- Is this person angry because I have chosen not to "rescue" him or her as I have in the past?
- Is this person angry because I will not agree to be victim to his or her neglect or abuse?

- Is this person angry because I refuse to support, encourage, or participate in his or her self-abusive or irresponsible behavior?
- Is this person angry because I cannot make him or her feel better or fix this person's problem for them?
  (These questions might be answered "yes" when I am refusing to play a co-dependent role in relationship to another. In this case, the anger is to be expected and not anything I can "fix.")

It is within your power to dismantle your side of the invisible barrier. Choose one issue with which you have resentment, and begin today. The exercise following this chapter has been designed to help you with the process.

Puzzle Piece #9: Remaining stuck in old behavior patterns
that feed resentment builds a wall that separates us.
I am choosing new patterns that liberate me from resentment.

This prayer repeated in most 12-step meetings is so appropriate for
the process of "recovery" from co-dependency:
"God, grant me the Serenity to accept the things I cannot change;
Courage to change the things I can;
and Wisdom to know the difference.
Living one day at a time, enjoying one moment at a time;
Accepting hardship as a pathway to peace;
Taking, as Jesus did, this sinful world as it is;
Not as I would have it;
Trusting that You will make all things right if I surrender to Your will;
So that I may be reasonably happy in this life
And supremely happy with You forever in the next. Amen."
Reinhold Niebuhr

"It is an honor to receive a frank reply."
Proverbs 24:26

*"Love forgets mistakes; nagging about them parts the best of
friends."*
Proverbs 17:9

Recovery from Co-dependency Exercise

Choose one thing for which you feel resentment toward your spouse.

What are you trying to make him or her do?
Which of your needs or wants are you holding him or her responsible for meeting?

What methods are you using to try to change him or her?

Name 3-5 results of your current methods of trying to effect change.

Is your current strategy producing the result you want?

Are you willing to try something different?

Start by doing the exercise on Identifying and Clearing Negative Projections from Chapter 10. Do it now.

If the resentment is because your spouse is not meeting his or her responsibilities the way you want him or her to, inwardly release them from your judgments and expectations.

If appropriate, ask for a mirroring session where you can express your concerns respectfully, without accusations. ("I feel" statements, only.) Make the purpose of the session simply to be heard, not the transformation of your spouse.

If your spouse has no interest in changing that behavior, then make a list of things *you* can do that will change *your* participation in the issue.
>   For example:
>   I will stop nagging about this issue.
>   I will look for alternative ways for this need to be met.
>   I will release him or her to their own learning process, rather than demanding that he or she be in a place that is comfortable to me.
>   I am open to other ideas of what I can appropriately do.
>   [Chapters 5 and 6 of Michele Weiner Davis's book, The Divorce

    Remedy, is full of ideas for different ways of doing things that
    effectively bring about healthy change. See Bibliography.]
    When we are open for new wisdom, we receive it one way or
    another.

I will make an appointment with a counselor to help me see new
options.

If the reason for the resentment is because you've been expecting
him or her to do something that can only be done for yourself, write
down a several possible steps that would assist you in taking
responsibility for things that are within your control. You are not
committing to do them, just writing them down.

    For example: If you want more self-assurance, would a martial
    arts class or a journaling workshop appeal to you? If you want
    more input financially, would purchasing a book such as Suze
    Orman's 9 Steps to Financial Freedom get you started? Are you
    willing to make a blueprint for the financial condition you desire
    and commit to building your belief in its fulfillment? [See Chapter
    2, "Blueprint for a SoulMate Marriage."] If you want more
    attention, are you willing to plan a mirroring session? Or, give
    more attention to yourself to increase your belief that you are
    worthy of attention?

If you are ready, choose one of those things and do it today, or
put it on the calendar to do at a specific time.

If appropriate, apologize to your spouse for asking him or her to be
responsible for something for which you need to be responsible. If
you can, share your plans.

    I can think of a hundred different circumstances that may be the
source of resentment in a relationship. The examples I've used only
cover a few, but I hope they give you some ideas about how to
proceed with your particular issues. I'm cheering for you!

"The only difference between rats and human beings is that human beings will go. . . down cheese-less tunnels forever because they're more intent on proving to themselves that they're right than they are in finding and eating the cheese! (Cheese being a great marriage.) When you do more of what hasn't been working, you not only fail to eliminate the problems in your life, you actually make things worse."
    Davis, Michele Weiner, (2001). The Divorce Remedy, p. 94-95

Chapter 12

Won by One

**"Have the relationship you always wanted with the partner
you already have."**
From *World Class Marriage* by Patty Howell and Ralph Jones

I am writing about my first marriage with some caution. The marriage ended after only four-and-one-half years with my husband's unexpected death. This occurred almost 35 years ago. There is no doubt that my memories are selective and possibly blurred. It seems unfair that he cannot tell his side. In spite of that, I tell this story because these particular events represent such an amazing awakening in my young life that they were vividly imprinted on my consciousness at the time they happened and the details have not altered with the passing of years. Since then the principles these events describe have been validated with my experience in other relationships and with the stories related by my clients, as well as by experienced, successful marriage therapists such as Michelle Weiner Davis.

I entered my first marriage at the age of eighteen (just six weeks short of nineteen) with a limited number of (mostly) defective relationship tools and unrealistic expectations. I was sure I could do a better job of being a wife and mother than I perceived my mother had done. (Forgive me, Mom!) I had vague imaginings of wonderful conversations over our dinner, (dinner would always be good and appreciated) quiet discussions about whatever issues arose, co-operative decision making, bodies attuned to each other, and adoring eyes gazing into mine. The smell of stale sweat, bouts of flu, mismatched sexual urges, days without hearing "I love you," out-and-out fights, and battles with depression never dared to spoil my dreams.

Since both of my husbands are named Jim, I'll reduce confusion by referring to the first as Jim G. Jim G. had no idea that the sweet girl he pledged to love forever came to him with almost 19 years worth of stored anger and an insatiable need to have someone prove that I was loved. Soon after we married, I forgot the admirable qualities that had attracted me to Jim G., and began to focus on (what I perceived as) his failings. The proof of his failings mostly consisted of my unhappiness. I thought I would be happy married to him. I wasn't. It must be his fault. It was that simple.

About six months into this union, it dawned on me that Jim G. was a lot like my father, and I was reacting to him in ways that echoed the most unappealing behaviors of my mother. I was horrified, but continued my campaign to make him shape up. It didn't work . . . surprised? We made it through two years with some uneventful days, and some days where my frustration and unhappiness erupted in a flow that seemed to drown us both. Nevertheless, with blithe naiveté, we decided that having a child was next on the list.

While awaiting the birth of this child, my fantasies were of a cherubic face gazing adoringly up into my eyes, a sweet smelling baby nestling into my arms while sleeping to the rhythm of my newly refinished heirloom rocker. Everyone would admire what a good mother I was. I took natural childbirth classes and, in every way I knew how to, prepared for a wonderful delivery.

The day Steven chose to arrive, there were nine babies delivered in two hours in two delivery rooms. The staff was short-tempered and decidedly impatient with a girl who thought she knew how to have a baby "naturally." The spinal block the doctor administered in spite of my protests only succeeded in stopping labor so Steven was delivered with forceps—a practice that, since, has been associated with attention deficit disorder and hyperactivity. After ADHD was discovered and named, it was confirmed that Steven had it, but as a baby, all I knew was he couldn't sleep more than 20 minutes at a time, wouldn't hold still in my arms, refused to be cuddled, and cried a lot.

Five months later, shortly after my 21st birthday, I was at the end of my rope. Neither my husband nor my child were giving me what I wanted. One day, face down on the floor, I begged God to help me. I was miserable. I couldn't make Jim G. or Steven act the way I wanted them to. The only thing left was for me to change. Would God please tell me how to change so that I could be happy? I would do anything! (I'm sure God smiled.)

Jim G. always got home at 5:30 p.m. *Except* when he called at 5:30 p.m. to tell me he was 200 miles away picking up some equipment that needed repair. He'd learned the hard way that I exploded when he was late, so he waited until the last minute to let me know. Although he never told me this, I imagine he had to brace himself to make those calls.

Two days after the desperate prayer-on-the-floor, dinner was ready to put on the table when the phone rang. Jim G. said that he was picking up broken equipment and wouldn't be home until after midnight. I clamped my jaws shut and told God, "If you're going to help me you'd better start now by giving me something to say that is different than my usual!" A moment later I was surprised to hear these words coming out of my mouth, "O.K., honey. I'll be glad to see you when you get home." Silence. Perhaps he thought he'd dialed the wrong number.

About 11:30 p.m. I was up with Steven when I heard Jim G.'s truck pull in the driveway. He bounded through the back door with a grin on his face and gave me a big hug saying, "Your words made me want to come home as fast as I could!" I was stunned. I'd just received my first lesson about being *Won by One*.

More lessons came. Jim G. worked six days a week, leaving home by 6:30 a.m. and (usually) coming back at 5:30 p.m. We spent most of the seventh day getting ready for, attending, and recovering from morning and evening church services. I was starving for attention. In the past, I had nagged until he agreed to take a Saturday off. Then, on the day for which I had begged, woke up with a migraine because I felt so guilty. I believed he was with me only to stop the nagging, not because he really wanted to be. After asking for guidance about this, I decided to switch my attention to being grateful for whatever time I had with him, rather than demanding time that he didn't want to give. I didn't tell him about this change of focus. [Review Chapter 5 about the magic of Gratitude.]

A month or so later, before leaving for work on a Saturday morning, Jim G. said, "I'm coming home at noon today. Is there anything you'd like to do?" Again, I was stunned! He came home, we puttered in the yard for awhile and then went for a drive or something. (That part is fuzzy.) I didn't get a migraine because I didn't feel guilty. He came home because he *wanted* to.

The next lesson I remember was about Jim G.'s lack of being affectionate. I wanted to hear, "I love you" often, and get unexpected bouquets of flowers, and be held just to be close, not because he wanted to make love. This didn't happen. It was one of the primary things I had tried to change about him. With plenty of help from above, I decided to look for ways he was demonstrating that he loved me, rather than demanding that his love be given the way I wanted it.

He had a thoroughly annoying habit of washing the car about 10 minutes before we were due to leave for church on Sunday morning. By this time, Peter had arrived. I had two babies plus myself to get ready. One Sunday morning I looked out the back window and saw him beginning to wash the car. The familiar anger began, but then I saw his behavior through a completely different filter. He was meticulous with his vehicles. He was proud of his family. He wanted to drive up to church (the center of our spiritual and social lives) in a clean car with his wife and two sons. It was his way of saying, "I love you." From that day on, every time he washed the car, my heart was warmed as I received the loving message he delivered in his "love language." (Remember Chapter 4!)

Our marriage wasn't perfect, but from the day of my desperate prayer to the day 18 months later when he unexpectedly died from an undiagnosed aortic aneurysm, our marriage (*and me*) had gone from constant tension to mostly happy and even, at times, playful. One aspect of my grief has always been the unanswered question, "If we had had more time, would we have gotten to the place where we could have talked about all this?" We never once discussed the changes that occurred. What was going on in his mind? Were some of the changes due to his conscious efforts, or were they a natural response to the changes *I* made in *me*? Would we eventually have learned the skills that Jim Landrum and I learned for more effective ways to communicate and resolve issues? I don't know. I *do* know, with *absolute certainty*, that the changes made in me brought about positive changes in the way we were together. One partner can be won into a better relationship by the changes deliberately chosen by the other.

Michele Weiner Davis, M.S.W. has devoted her life to experimenting with ways that marriages can be saved. I tend to believe, (and most agree) that it's ideal for both partners to be actively engaged in learning skills that will improve their marriage, but Michele often prefers working with only one partner when the other has already left the marriage or is convinced it is hopeless. The number and variety of success stories told in her book, <u>The Divorce Remedy</u> and the subsequent <u>Divorce Busting</u> series document the effectiveness of one person who is willing to change.

Every relationship tends to get stuck in predictable patterns of behavior. We tend to play off of each other with repetition that is maddening. He says this. She replies with that. He stomps off to the garage. She calls a girlfriend to complain. There's three hours of silence, (or three days, take your pick). He breaks the deadlock with an invitation to a movie. She acquiesces. Both pretend everything is fine again. Neither want to start it up. 'Til the next time he says something. She replies . . . .

As described in Chapter 8 (Velcro), these patterns build a barrier to intimacy, prevent healthy resolution, and cause amnesia in regard to why two people originally loved each other. If it becomes a pattern of chronic conflict, or if the silence to avoid conflict goes on long enough, the marriage, though appearing intact, has an empty core. One partner may elect to leave.

It isn't at all unusual for one partner to want to work on improving the marriage while the other one doesn't. The biggest mistake for the willing partner can make is to wait until the other is also ready. That strategy leaves the unwilling partner in control of the marriage while the willing partner becomes more frustrated. The one who is ready can, with Michelle's book or in a skills based marriage seminar, be coached about how to change his or her participation in the relationship. It's true with marriages, as well as computers—when you change the input, the output also changes. Marriages are a closed system . . . when one part of it moves, the whole is affected.

I'm not saying that a happy outcome is guaranteed. The unwilling partner is an individual with the power of choice. His or her choice may be determinedly against the marriage, no matter what. But miracles frequently happen, even when the unwilling spouse has already physically and emotionally left the marriage—even when he or she is involved with someone new.

If you are willing but your spouse isn't, buy one of Ms. Davis's books immediately. In easy reading, everyday language she maps out simply structured strategies for identifying what is happening, experimenting with change on your part, and documenting the results. The key is to be truly dedicated to improving or restoring the marriage and be prepared for a long-term process. One of my clients accepted the challenge. I'll call him Sam.

By his own admission, as a husband Sam was over-bearing, controlling, sometimes obnoxious, and loudly combative. For the first several years of their marriage, Rose, his wife, was somewhat timid and compliant. After their two children were in school, Rose held a very responsible job in a large organization. Her self confidence grew. She attempted to be more assertive, wanted her ideas to be considered, tried to be a more equal partner, and longed for her wishes to matter. Her efforts and needs were ignored. Sam ratcheted up his pattern of control. She rebelled by withholding sex. He reacted with anger. He embarrassed her by acting nasty with her friends, embarrassing her in social situations, fighting frequently with her and with the children, and generally being unpleasant to be around. She avoided him whenever possible, refused to be in public with him, stopped entertaining in their home, and began sleeping downstairs on the couch. After many months of this escalating stalemate, Rose announced to Sam and the (now) teenage children that she wanted a divorce.

Although Sam did not want a divorce, he is a businessman who is accustomed to being logical and adjusting to changing conditions. He attempted to adjust to this change by enrolling in a divorce recovery support group although they were still living under the same roof. One foggy morning he went to the beach near his home, sat on a rock, and allowed the despair that had been gathering for many months to wash over him like the waves over the sand at his feet. He asked God for help.

Within a few days he read an article where Diane Sollee's web site, (www.smartmarriages.com) was mentioned. He got online and asked for a referral to a class or counselor in his area that might be able to help him. His request was forwarded to me. We met a few days later

From the beginning Sam has been candid about the nature of his behavior toward Rose and insatiable in his determination to educate himself about how to restore and keep a *good* marriage. At first, we met every week. He kept notes during the week so he could report to me what happened with Rose since we last met. He'd tell me not only what Rose did, but what he did. We talked about events he saw as key from their exchanges over the last few years. I helped him interpret what I thought her behavior meant, or share how I would respond if Jim treated me in the ways he described. I occasionally caught a glimpse of how deeply he was hurting, but for the most part, he responded to these lessons with quick, humorous quips or lightly sarcastic exaggerations.

Sam asked me frequently how long this would take, and I had to answer, "As long as it takes." When he finished our book, he moved on to Ms. Davis's <u>The Divorce Remedy</u>, and then worked his way through our entire marriage library. He began to report small changes in Rose . . . minute changes, really, but, together, we were looking for any gleam of hope.

After several weeks the children pointed out to their mother, "Dad's changed. Are you still getting a divorce?" He was encouraged when she evaded an answer.

A month later he asked what he could do to help prepare for a neighborhood block party. She told him. He graciously did what she suggested and went out of his way to be pleasant to the neighbors. Later she thanked him for his help.

A holiday approached. He asked if they were going to the cousins to celebrate. (The previous year he'd gone to a friend's, she to the cousins, alone.) He told her he'd like to go with her and would be willing to be instructed by her about how to behave. She only said she didn't want him to spend all evening watching <u>Twilight Zone</u> reruns (his favorite) with the kids. They negotiated the amount of time he could absent himself and he kept his agreement with her.

After several months of inching along, she consented to a sandwich together at a local bakery. Since they hadn't eaten out alone together for ten years, this was a major breakthrough!

A month later, she agreed to go with him and another couple to see a movie. Although she disliked the movie, this also was a biggie.

One morning while the whole family was eating breakfast and preparing to leave, their daughter asked Rose, "Do you still love Dad?" Rose answered simply, "Yes" and turned away. Talk of moving out and divorce had stopped.

By this time, I saw Sam about once a month. He was on track so we conferred about the encounters that had happened since our last meeting. It was going much more slowly than he wanted, but although he was impatient, he maintained his steadfast focus on the goal and had incredible patience with Rose.

She decided to redecorate a downstairs bath. We took that as major encouragement . . . she was investing creativity and energy into their shared home. Historically, Sam had been rather tight with money. The house had been neglected, needing repairs. The carpet was worn and walls needed repainting. Before launching his marriage restoration project, Sam had withheld funds for these things as punishment for her withdrawal. I shared that for most women, our homes are an extension of ourselves. He began to see the condition of the house as a reflection of the neglect of his wife. He loosened his hold on the money, and Rose began planning for new carpeting and paint. When I heard this, I assured Sam that the tide had turned. A woman does not invest herself in a house that she intends to leave to a former husband!

Although Sam was quite comfortable financially, he'd been looking for a new direction for his gift for business ventures. His quest led to a specialized kind of real estate investment. He shared what he was learning with Rose. She became interested. He was learning to use "team" language with her, rather than "I decided…" or "This is what I'm going to do."

At our last appointment, Sam and Rose had enjoyed dinner out with her cousin and spouse. They had not been out socially like that for more than ten years. They had such a good time that before the evening was over, someone suggested the four of them plan a weekend get-away soon. Sam held his breath. Rose smiled and said, "That would be fun."

One of the books Sam read was Harville Hendrix's, **<u>Getting the Love You Want.</u>** We *highly* recommend it. Dr. Hendrix does an outstanding job of explaining about the unresolved childhood issues that we unconsciously bring to marriage for resolution. Sam realized that his parents had been emotionally unavailable to him. His home was undemonstrative and pretty silent. He never learned how to be warm and receptive on an intimate level. One of the reasons he married Rose was because her family had such rousing conversations around the dinner table. On an unconscious level, he thought Rose would provide that kind of family for him. He discounted the effect on her of his harshness and coldness toward her needs. In doing the work needed to restore her love for him, he is becoming the man he needed for a father. The traits of sensitivity, thoughtfulness, gentle humor, and kindness are being developed in him. His children have noticed. There is much less fighting between the four of them. The children have made no secret of the fact that they are rooting for a fully restored marriage between Mom and Dad. They want to see them affectionate with each other, like they remember from years ago.

Although she still sleeps on the sofa, it's only a matter of time before their marriage is completely healed. The kind of dedicated, patient, loving pursuit that Sam has done over the past year cannot be resisted indefinitely. Love is like that. Irresistible. He is a living testimony to the power of being *Won by One*.

Update: Several months after this was written, I got an excited e-mail from Sam. Rose had moved back into their (redecorated) bedroom! *And* their relationship was again, gratefully, sexual! Hurrah! Great work, Sam!

Puzzle Piece #9: SoulMate Responsibility
Change what is within *your* control.

"It's never too late to save your marriage."
Michelle Weiner Davis, M.S.W., www.divorcebusting.com.

"Your godly life will speak better than any words."
I Peter 3:1

"Be patient and you will finally win, for a soft tongue can break hard bones."
Proverbs 25:15

Chapter 13

For Those Who Are "Blending"

*"Families are flawed, complex, intense organic units
whose members often fail each other in important ways.
But family affection is the glue that holds lives together."*
[Pipher, Mary, Ph.D., (1996). The Shelter of Each Other,
Rebuilding Our Families,
p. 225-226. New York: Ballantine Books.**]**

Note: Except for the title of this chapter, I studiously avoid the words "blended family." The term is ludicrous! We aren't a milk-shake. We don't homogenize any more than a nuclear family is "blended." We are a complex mix of unique individuals who have been brought into relationship through various circumstances and hope we can support and love each other in healthy and meaningful ways.

The "step" in "stepfamily" refers to one person stepping into the role of another who is no longer there. The term was created when far more persons were left without a partner due to death and the demands of life dictated that the missing spouse be replaced in order to share the work load. Stepfamily, step-father, step-mother, etc are not ideal labels in these times, but until we find more suitable terms, I believe they are more accurate than "blended."

You know you are a stepfamily if:
1. Your last name is Smith and your children's last names are Johnson and Cooper.

2. You think your child is basically a good kid—but his or her child is a real problem!
3. You have found yourself, occasionally, feeling nostalgic about the "good old days" as a single parent.
4. You hear, "You're not my mom (dad)!"
5. Your child has four separate birthday parties and you travel to six different houses on Christmas.
6. You received a family law summons from an ex-spouse before your honeymoon was over.
7. You now see Cinderella's stepmother and her three ugly stepsisters as negative stereotypes.
8. You struggle.
[Excerpted from "Realistic Expectations of Remarriage," an article by Steve Sposato at www.steplife.com.]

Jim and I have felt so much sorrow over our failure to recognize or adequately meet our children's needs during the traumatic upheaval in their lives created by our marriage. We have been speaking about the healing of our SoulMate love for several years, but only recently, with great hesitation, agreed to speak to a step-family support group about the challenges of parenting in a step-family. Mostly we told them about all the hurtful things we did out of ignorance and blissful naiveté. By the time we found out that most step-families thrive with very different rules than biological families, and made some drastic changes, our children had suffered—some of them terribly.

In our defense, when we needed them, there were only a handful of books on the subject of stepfamily dynamics. Those brave authors were just beginning to expose the unique and, until recently, unrecognized foundational differences between a traditional, nuclear, biologically created family and a step or "blended" family. One of the counselors we saw for a few visits was in a second marriage with "yours, mine, and ours." The therapist gave Jim some very valuable feedback about his relationship with Jimmy, but didn't have a clue about where I should fit in.

If you don't "get" anything else about this chapter, "get" this: The guidelines for successfully "blending" two families are as different from what makes a biological family work as the difference between good recipes for beef stew and lasagna. Both recipes require planning, attention to details, good seasoning, and a caring cook, but in order for each entree to be tasty, very different ingredients and cooking methods are needed.

In one major respect, we were fortunate. We did not bring into our marriage the wounds of a previous, failed relationship. We did not have to cope with hostile former spouses, angry former in-laws, or an impersonal legal system dictating custody arrangements or visiting agreements. I can only *try* to fathom the additional stresses that those factors place on the already fractured structure of a stepfamily.

We did, however, have our former spouses' parents and other extended family members who, understandably, wanted to maintain contact with Jim and me, as well as with the children. I remember when Dixie's family visited us soon after we married. I was so aware of their graciousness to me in spite of their grief over Dixie's death. We all tried so hard it was exhausting. I remember Jim, the girls, and Dixie's family spending a lot of time recalling funny stories about her. It was healing for them. I didn't begrudge them the healing, but felt excluded, not because they were shunning me, but by the long history they all shared together. I was envious.

The complexity of the extended family of steps is mind-boggling. In a first marriage, adjustments owing to differing family patterns and demands of in-laws are often difficult. In a stepfamily, the issues multiply exponentially. For some, the complexity of biological and step relatives is mind-boggling. More and more often, the grandparents of the stepchildren have also divorced and remarried! It could be hard to find a piece of paper large enough to hold the diagram of the family tree!

In our case, the number of mouths to feed doubled instantly. I felt snowed by the job of simply keeping enough food in the house and planning meals. A few months after we married, I spent days planning out menus for 4 weeks, organizing the recipes in a notebook, and making grocery lists for each of 4 weeks. I planned to rotate the same menus each month. I made one mistake. Every fourth day or so, I left an evening meal open for eating up leftovers; but there weren't any! I was accustomed to cooking only every other day or so. Between the extra bodies and boys entering puberty with un-fill-able stomachs, the cooking seemed to take five times more effort than before. I resented it.

We took the equity from the sale of Jim's house and doubled the square footage of my house—another mistake. The home was functional and beautiful, but my children never surrendered emotional ownership of the house and Jim and his children never really felt like it was theirs. Some time later, we learned that it works better to sell both homes and buy one that is neutral territory for everyone.

In addition to the surprise stresses of extended family, cooking, and house ownership, there were more subtle unrealistic expectations that created hurt and anger as they surfaced over time. I expected my life to get easier, now that I had SoulMate, lover, and best friend with whom to share responsibilities. I thought my days of repairing sprinklers, installing curtain rods, or disciplining strong willed boys by myself were over. I expected my boys to be happy for me. Jim thought his girls would be my friends and Jimmy would welcome me as "Mom."

Jim had carried most of the practical burdens of household management and the parenting of Jimmy during the long years of Dixie's illness. He was relieved to turn the bill paying over to me. He expected me to have the same relationship with Jimmy that Dixie had enjoyed. He was sure I would adore Jimmy as did the rest of his family. I expected Jim to see past the hostility of my boys toward him, and value them for the great young men they obviously were under their sullen exteriors. We both expected the children to get along and love each other because *we* were happy. They barely knew each other! They fought about everything! They had no choice in this! Years later they confided that they sometimes had late night confabs commiserating with each other on the only subject about which they could agree—how terrible we were!

Another deeply hidden unrealistic expectation took longer to surface. I believed that my first attempts at "family" were flawed. I thought I'd lost my chance to be a truly great wife and mother because my first husband died, taking my dream with him. I had done the best I knew how to do as a single mom, certainly giving it all I had to give, but now I had a second chance! I wanted to "make" this family perfect! Because I didn't have healthy communication skills or an understanding of what makes a stepfamily work, I did what I knew how to do: I planned elaborate birthday celebrations for each member of the family. I cooked grand meals. I shopped for great gifts. I expended a huge amount of energy on how the family looked from the outside. I guess I believed that if we looked good, the inner bonding and love would follow. Instead, the wounds, resentments, and unmet expectations corroded our chances from the inside out.

As I write this list, I am chagrinned at the level of unreality and thoughtless insensitivity we demonstrated toward each other, yes, but primarily toward our children. I was so love-starved that, in retrospect, I see that I essentially abandoned my sons to spend as much time as possible with Jim. Recently one of them told me that at that time he believed he was no longer important to me—to the point of being expendable. I thought I was paying attention to them, but, obviously, not to the degree they needed. I was oblivious to the grief my sons were experiencing over the loss of the three-some that we had been for so long. Later they told me that, for all of their remembered life to that point, it had been Mom, Steve, and Pete against the world.

In talking with other step families, we hear that it is altogether too common for the grief being experienced by the children to be overlooked or judged as unnecessary because the parents are so joyful about finding love again.

We had been married 8 or 9 years and the worst of our nightmare was over. I was beginning to recognize how lost Steve and Pete had been in the chaos of those years. Jim was invited to sing the National Anthem at a California Angels game and was given a few complimentary tickets. I love to hear him sing, but told him to invite those who would appreciate seeing the Angels in person more than I would. I called Steven and asked to take him out to dinner. He was surprised. Where was Jim? Didn't I want to go to the game, too? When I answered, "I'd rather spend the evening with you, tonight" he nearly cried. He was about 23 years old and on his own. He answered, "You can't know how good it feels to hear you want to be with me more than Jim, for once."

They have told me that they wanted me to be happy, and didn't really begrudge me a husband, but felt as though their place with me disappeared in the transaction. At a time when they needed more time and individual attention, I gave them less. I made the mistake of thinking my relationship with them was proven and secure, so my energy went into trying to build the new relationships with Jim and his children. I forgot my first priority, which was the welfare of my own sons.

Even though I wasn't aware of how much more of me they needed during those years, I had years of precious memories and bonding experiences with them that made it possible for me to see beyond their acting out. Jim had no history with them, so was impatient and offended by one's rudeness and the other's defiance and trouble making. He was seeing them only at their worst. I had not given birth to Jimmy, had not watched him learn to walk, or celebrated his learning of language. When he shared some boyish treasure with me, I was touched; but, when he whined or pestered, I was annoyed. I felt guilty and helpless one night when he, face down on his bedroom carpet, wailed "I want my Mommy!" over and over for at least 30 minutes. I knew it wasn't for me his little broken heart was crying.

As the stepparent, we have no history and no bonding from which to draw tolerance or to temper our irritation. It is so classic as to be a rule that the stepparent always sees what the stepchild needs more clearly than the biological parent. Children were meant to be reared by biological parents for this very reason . . . the "rules" are softened by the loving bond. That bond is absent in the step-relationship.

A Step-Dog?

The issue of a lack of bonding even extended to our family dog. Lady, our exuberant boxer, had been a full member of our family for about 8 years before the Landrum bunch joined us. Lady loved the extra attention, but my boys resented Jimmy for calling her "his" dog. I was hurt by Jim's irritation with her shedding and his disgust at the fleas she introduced to our carpet. I didn't like shedding or fleas, either, but accepted the extra vacuuming and flea treatments as part of the price I willingly paid for her valued membership in the family.

Now, we laugh about an incident with Lady the first Christmas we were all together. Teri, Jim's oldest daughter, had married the year before. In a grand effort to give her support to the "new" family's first Christmas, she made each family member a red Christmas stocking. They were filled with fruits, nuts, little gifts, and each was topped with a small package of gourmet Famous Amos Chocolate Chip Cookies. The stockings were stored in a large brown grocery sack in our bedroom, waiting to be hung over the fireplace.

Jim and I returned home late one evening to find a trail of empty stockings, oranges, and nuts from our bedroom to the doggy door at the other end of the house. Jim was furious. He found Lady shirking in the shadows of the patio, fully aware that she was in big trouble! Torn Famous Amos wrappers testified to the fact that she had eaten every cookie from every stocking. As he marched around the yard picking up bits of evidence, he was "yelling" in a heavy stage whisper to avoid rousing sleeping children or neighbors, "BAD DOG! VERY BAD DOG!" I knew he wanted to swat her but wouldn't dare. I was in the house, chuckling. He spent the next several days trying to track down identical packages of cookies so he could reconstruct the stockings. The cookies were outrageously expensive, but he didn't want Teri to think we were uncaring or unappreciative of her efforts toward family solidarity. It was many years before he could tell Teri the story and laugh.

Lady lived with our "blended" family for 5 more years. After her death everyone missed her, but even so, no one grieved her loss more than Steven, Peter, and I. We had bonded with her as a puppy, and had 8 more years of history with her than the other half of the family.

What began as little scratches here and there, eventually became a gaping wound from which the family nearly died. By 1984-1985, I had gained nearly 100 pounds from a raging eating disorder and was clinically depressed; Jim and I could hardly be in the same room without fighting; Karen was struggling her way into a shaky adulthood; Steven had been expelled from several high schools and was using drugs; Peter was withdrawn, going about his life in isolation, head down against the storm; and Jimmy fluctuated between compulsive demands for one thing after another and grand tantrums of the type usually seen in toddlers. It was about this time that Jim's threat to divorce me occurred. Ultimately, that crisis led to our seriously looking for help and the slow process that resulted in the saving of our marriage and the eventual healing of our family.

Most of this agony could have been avoided if we had known the one primary principle that works for most stepfamilies—the concept of biologically driven parenting. In Chapter 23, "Going to the Movies," I shared about eventually resigning from my role as Jimmy's mom. At the time it seemed like a drastic, horribly painful step. We thought it was necessary because Jim and I had been so "bad," such "failures" at working together as Jimmy's parents. Now we know that the original expectation that I would fully be Jimmy's parent, was unreasonable. It very, very rarely works.

Biologically driven parenting is promoted by the Stepfamily Association of America as well as a growing number of experts on stepfamily dynamics. Biologically driven parenting is characterized by these practices:

1. The biological parent is always the primary parent and always the source of any discipline even if the stepparent thinks he or she doesn't discipline enough!

2. The biological parent and the stepparent discuss the parenting plans in private, perhaps even take a parenting class together. They agree on specific house rules and consequences of misbehavior. Ideally *both* agree, but the final decision is always the biological parent's.

3. House rules are written down for the benefit of parents and child.

4. The biological parent takes the lead in dealing with the child. The stepparent backs up the biological parent so the child cannot pit them against each other.

5. The biological parent follows through consistently with the plans agreed upon, first of all for the benefit of the child, but also so that the stepparent is not placed in the intolerable position of being an adult, helplessly at the mercy of a misbehaving child.

6. The stepparent backs up the written rules as a messenger, not the source of the discipline. The rules are referred to as "your Mom's (Dad's) rules" not "our rules."

7. Spouses reevaluate parenting regularly, keeping each other "in the loop" and cooperating respectfully with each other.

8. Lapses of discipline, or annoying infractions of house rules are issues that are settled first between the spouses, and then between the biological parent and child. The stepparent curbs the desire to control, scold, or discipline the stepchild.

9. Frustrations and upsets are discussed between spouses within the format of a mirroring session, *first* hearing each other's feelings, *then* problem solving. All the rules of respectful communication are especially important in this process because the biological parent is deeply, and instinctively protective of the child if that child is attacked. Most *adults* are defensive if their parenting skills are attacked, as well. [Respectful communication is practiced with the ex-spouse, as well. The tools that work to build a great marriage also increase the chances of having a sane, workable relationship with your child's other biological parent. Just as dealing with the child is the biological parent's responsibility, all communication with the other biological parent (ex-spouse) is the responsibility of the former spouse, not the new husband's or wife's responsibility.]

10. The pace of developing the relationship between stepchild and stepparent (or stepchild to stepchild) must be dictated by the child, not forced by the stepparent. Certainly invitations for a shared activity or caring questions and conversations are offered, but the child is given time and freedom to respond when ready without undue pressure to "produce" a good relationship with the stepparent on command. Of course, common courtesy and respect are expected of everyone in the household.

I thought my heart would break when I relinquished my role as traditional mom to Jimmy. The change in dynamic had almost instantaneous benefits, however.

1. I no longer had the responsibility of trying to figure out what was best for Jimmy. That was now entirely up to Jim. My only responsibility was to work with Jim when decisions concerning Jimmy directly affected me. An essential part of our agreement was that I would not even offer advice or suggestions unless Jim asked for them. It wasn't long before I began to feel relieved that the responsibility was no longer mine.

2. A huge source of conflict was eliminated between Jim and me. It took a while for us to regain our trust in each other . . . trust that we would each honor the new "rules" to which we had agreed. There were slips, but overall, we experienced an instant, gigantic leap forward in the regaining of our love.

3. The problems Jimmy was having could no longer be blamed on me. Without the struggles being focused on me, and what I was doing to cause problems with Jimmy, Jim soon realized that Jimmy had some needs that were not being met by his parenting practices. He was eager to get help. He began implementing an active parenting plan that provided far more healthy guidance for Jimmy.

Over years, the stepparent may or may not gradually begin to meld into a more traditional parental role. The younger the child, the sooner the stepparent *may* be able to assume a semi-parental role, with the approval of the biological parent. This is becoming known as "graduated parenting." The stepparent's first priority is to offer opportunities for bonding with the child. The child is ultimately in charge of how fast those efforts will be accepted. With some children it's almost immediate. With others a bond develops over many years—or never. The stepparent only assumes a more traditional role of authority/parent as the relationship with the child builds. A general rule of thumb is that it takes up to the same number of years to "blend" a family as the age of the child when the marriage took place.

I spent a day with Teri collecting medical records and getting pre-op tests shortly before her back surgery. Before we walked into the first of several doctor's offices, she said, "Would it be O.K. if I just introduce you as my mom? You *feel* like a mom to me today, and I'd be proud to introduce you as my mom, Nancy." Yes!

Dixie was gravely ill during Karen's early teens and died when Karen was 16 years old. I was helping Karen as she was recuperating from Alyssa's difficult birth. She said something like, "I can barely remember my mom before she was sick. You feel like a mom to me. You're the one who's been there to answer questions about being pregnant and nursing. You're there when I have questions or want guidance. You're a mom to me." Sigh.

Steven was 15 years old when we married. Just before his 30th birthday, Steven said something like this to Jim during a treasured conversation held in "guy" territory (the garage) late one night: "You did the best job of being a stepfather that I could ever have asked for. None of my problems were your fault. I'm sorry I hurt you. I'm glad you're there for my Mom. I love you and respect you. I'm grateful you've been there for me, too."

When Peter calls home, he and Jim have long conversations whether I'm here or not. When we made the 300-mile trip to see Pete's graduation from the California Highway Patrol Academy, Jim's hug and "Your father would be so proud of your today" brought tears to Peter's eyes. Pete has told me several times how much respect he has for Jim.

Soon after I "resigned" as a primary parent to Jimmy, I gave him the option of calling me by my first name. As of today, he is 28 years old and I am still "Mom." I feel so blessed to have his love and loyalty after all we put him through. And I'm the one he knows will bake his favorite chocolate chip cookies (not Famous Amos!).

For me, a large part of the healing was grieving the loss of the family I *thought* we would be. We would never be a "normal" family. I, again, had blown the chance to be a perfect wife and mother of a perfect family. It's taken time and distance for me to see that there *are no perfect families*. Maybe there are no "normal" families, either. There are just families . . . biological, step, happy, sad, dysfunctional, and healing. Grieving the loss of the *fantasy* made room for the wonderful *reality* of the family that we are.

There *is* hope for stepfamilies.

Strategies that enable a stepfamily to succeed are

Different than for a biological or nuclear family.

Accepting and co-operating with that truth minimizes our struggles.

A step-father reports:

"I began to feel like a permanent assistant coach. I was there on the sidelines, there at halftime, but ultimately, I made none of the decisions. I had to accept that they weren't my children...I had to focus on stewardship and service, not ownership. I also had to accept that I didn't have a fan club.

The kids would never run to greet me: 'Daddy's here!'"

[Reported by a step-father in a support group where Jim and I spoke.]

"The fruit of the Spirit is love, joy, peace,

patience, kindness, goodness,

faithfulness, gentleness, and self-control."

Galatians 5:22-23

Note from Nancy: This sequel was written at the same time Jim and I wrote **How to Stay Married & Love It!** published in 2002. **EVEN MORE!** has only been available as an e-book until now. As I re-read it, I'm grateful to find all of the concepts and stories to be as true now as when I wrote it!

Recently (2020) I was thrilled when **Stepping TwoGether: Building a Strong Stepfamily** was published, fulfilling a dream of many years. **Stepping TwoGether** combines stories of real stepfamilies, including ours, with the research validated strategies that have been proven to help stepfamilies succeed. Available from Amazon.com, **Stepping TwoGether** delivers much more thorough information, is easy to read, and I believe you'll find it to be far more helpful than this single chapter!

Puzzle Piece #10:

SoulMate Romance

Chapter 14

The Recipe for Romance Cake

**"Men always want to be a woman's first love.
Women have a more subtle instinct:
what they like is to be a man's last romance."
Oscar Wilde**

I cannot imagine any artificially altered state that could be more intoxicating than falling in love. I think we all want it to last forever—the glow, the intensity, the sense of coming home, the certainty of belonging. It is the belief that this "in love-ness" is forever that gives us the courage to commit to a lifetime together.

But there can only be one first kiss, one first honeymoon, one first love-making, one first time you set up house together . . . those are the parts of love that are featured in the movies . . . but, eventually the daily-ness of life begins to invade the euphoria. He leaves the cap off of the toothpaste, she leaves her underwear drying over the shower door . . . and so the work of learning what we need to learn from each other has begun.

Yet, we've all seen them—the white-haired couples who still walk hand in hand, talking and smiling with each other. How do some couples stay "in love" for life? What is their secret recipe for romance longevity?

The recipe for SoulMate romance has many ingredients that are rarely shown in the latest date movie. They are simple things that must be kept on hand in every SoulMate marriage—the attitudes and practices that have been described in both "How to…" books.

Every time Jim comes home when he said he would, or plants a kiss on the back of my neck before he leaves, or asks for a date to tell me about an issue, or mirrors my feelings, or gives me his full attention, or offers to walk the dog when he knows it's my turn, or vacuums the living room, or plans a special date with me, or gladly surrenders all of his income to the family account, or buys life insurance to make sure I'll be O.K. if he dies, or compliments my appearance, he is mixing a tried-and-true recipe for SoulMate romance!

Every time I buy one See's dark chocolate covered cherry and leave it on his pillow, or greet him at the door with a warm hug and kiss, or rinse his dirty dishes for him, or bake cornbread, or tell him he's my Rock of Gibraltar, or cut his hair, or speak truthfully about an annoyance, or translate a sarcastic comment into a respectful one, or plan a surprise for him, or warmly respond to his seduction, or comfort his venting without offering unsolicited advice, or express confidence in him, I am following a tried-and-true recipe for SoulMate romance!

The Basic Ingredients for the Romance Cake are provided when I:
    Speak truthfully and respectfully,
    Communicate my feelings and needs appropriately,
    Listen to my partner empathically,
    Handle my anger responsibly,
    Keep my 2-year-old under control,
    Comfort without "fixing" my partner's feelings,
    Disconnect from co-dependency and assume full responsibility
    for myself,

Choose beliefs that support life-long romance,
Consistently make our relationship a high priority,
Participate in creating a romantic, as well as practical, SoulMate
Blueprint, [74]
Give my partner my whole-hearted commitment for life.

The Spices in the Romance Cake are added when I:
Communicate love in my partner's love language,
Am lavish with my "deposits" to our bank account,
Appreciate and acknowledge my partner often.

The Leavening

Leavening is an agent such as yeast or baking powder that adds lightness to the batter by incorporating air. The leavening agents for this very special cake are regular dates—not a date for mirroring an issue—but for the primary purpose of being together, talking together, laughing, and enjoying one another. For some SoulMates this means a regular, weekly date night. In our opinion, once a week is a minimum. Dates offer a welcome change of pace from the heavier routines of life. They remind us that we like each other's company. Dates give us a chance to laugh and giggle, be young and silly. They provide relief from the chores of life. A date adds lightness—leavening to the mix, as well as an opportunity to discuss shared concerns without distractions.

Some wives complain that dates only happen when they plan them. They want the experience of being taken. The romance of the evening is dampened when the wife must arrange for a baby-sitter and make all the decisions about when and where to go, what to do. If both agree that a regular date night will help to build a SoulMate relationship, perhaps both can agree to alternate responsibility for making the arrangements and decisions. The most important thing, however, is that you go!

If one forgets, the other can ask to be mirrored about his or her feelings about the date being forgotten. Do not resort to nagging, or any of the other defective communication tools. When the next date

---

[74] Chapter 29.

night comes, dress for it, and if your partner has forgotten, quietly and to the best of your ability, without rancor, say, "I really wanted to be with you tonight. Since our date has been forgotten, I'm going to go out by myself for a few hours because I need a break from the routine *and* I need time to calm down from my disappointment that keeping the agreement to spend special time together does not appear to be a high priority. I'll be home by ______o'clock." (And do be home when you said you would. SoulMates do not punish a broken agreement by breaking another agreement. That will only build the wall of resentment higher rather than working to remove it altogether.)

When you get home, or at the next opportunity, ask for a date to mirror the issue. Keep in mind that the long-range goal is that a regular, pleasurable date time become an event that is happily anticipated by both. It would be counter-productive to make the emotional scene so unpleasant that dates become a dreaded chore rather than a welcome interlude. If an apology is given, quickly accept it. Drop the issue and start again.

We take one day a week that is just for us. "Have to" errands are kept to a bare minimum. Our day off frequently begins with breakfast in a favorite restaurant. It often includes an hour or two of playing table games in a park or mall (depending on the weather.) We may attend a movie, or go home for an afternoon "nap" (smile). We may return home to work individually for an hour or two and then drive down to the beach for a "sunset special" dinner. This week we included a slow walk in a beautiful park while we brainstormed the skits and agenda for our first ever Workshop II. Often, during a busy week, subjects of importance get shelved until our day together when we can discuss them unhurriedly, without pressure.

It would be smart, at least some of the time, to plan dates around your partner's interests. For a wife who is uninterested in basketball to purchase tickets for your husband's favorite team as one of your date nights, could not be mistaken for anything other than a love-gift spoken in his language! For a husband to plan a date around one of your wife's interests is a clear message, boldly delivered, that she is loved!

We occasionally plan surprise days for each other, sometimes to celebrate a birthday, but usually for no reason at all. Some time ago, Jim let me know he was planning a day for me. (He lets me know in advance because a lot of the fun for me is anticipating it!) The morning of the special day, he told me what kind of clothes to wear (casual) and to bring a dress-up outfit along. We got on the freeway, heading for (I found out later) an ocean-side restaurant in Malibu. Jim put a cassette in the player and said, "This is what I want to say to you today." The words of the song began:

> "Tomorrow mornin' if you wake up and the sun does not appear, I will be here; If in the darkness we lose sight of love, hold my hand and have no fear, 'cause I will be here; When you feel like bein' quiet, when you need to speak your mind, I will listen, and I will be here; When the laughter turns to cryin' through the winnin', losin' and tryin' we'll be together, 'cause I will be here."[75]

My makeup was ruined! But I wasn't about to let *that* spoil my perfect day. After breakfast he took me to a shop in Santa Monica that specialized in antique quilts he thought I would enjoy seeing. Then we wandered through an intriguingly different shopping mall (something he would *only* do out of *great* love for me!). We played some table games, changed clothes in a public restroom, and ended the day by going to the theater to see a light romantic comedy.

There have been many surprise-days since that one, both given and received, some much more loosely planned than that one, and some just as elaborate. Books can be found in your local library or bookstore with great date ideas. Your newspaper or regional magazines often have articles about local events or places of interest. Jim and I each have a file where we keep ideas for future dates. For example, during an otherwise ordinary day off, Jim once surprised me with a visit to a fantastic garden nursery that he learned about from a newspaper article.

---

[75] Words and Music by Steven Curtis Chapman, <u>The Wedding Collection</u>, Word Music. 1993.

When one of us plans a surprise agenda for the other, the day is especially treasured. The fact that either Jim or I must plan ahead, taking into consideration the interests and desires of the other, makes the outing a successful love-gift before it has even begun! We both relish knowing about a surprise date ahead of time so we can savor the awareness of being very loved.

Our twentieth anniversary is coming up in a few weeks. We don't have any set pattern about things like this, but this year, I volunteered to plan our celebration. I have reservations for a three-night stay in a seaside town far enough away to be off our beaten track. I have some places in mind to visit and possible restaurants chosen.

Last night, while driving with my sister, she said, "You have to hear this song. It's incredible!" She started the compact disk:

"Miles of loneliness now make perfect sense here beside you
Tears like waterfalls. It was worth them all just to find you.
And yours are the last arms I'll run to . . .
Now I know how the river feels when it reaches the sea.
It finally finds the place it was always meant to be,
Holding fast, home at last, knowing the journey's through.
I'm here with you. I know how the river feels."[76]

I instantly knew I had to tape a copy to play for Jim on the way to our anniversary celebration. Today my sister, who seems to know all the popular artists and has a fantastic C.D. collection, helped me select and record a variety of love songs, starting with "I Know How the River Feels." Doesn't it sound romantic? Jim will *love* it! And we've been married *20 years!*

How do we know we'll still feel like being romantic on our thirtieth or even fiftieth anniversaries? Because we know the recipe for being "in love" and we are both committed to mixing all the

---

[76] "I Know How the River Feels" performed by Diamond Rio on their album, <u>Unbelievable</u>, produced by Michael D. Clute and Diamond Rio. Words and music written by Steven Dale Jones and Amy Powers, 1996. Island Bound Music, Inc., Famous Music Corporation/Powers That Be Music.

essential ingredients for as long as we both live! "Love is a living thing. If you nurture it, it grows. If you neglect it, it dies."[77]

The Frosting:

A cake without frosting is incomplete! Romance without love-making is also incomplete!   Today, a sexual encounter can happen nearly anywhere, anytime, with anyone, and with very little prelude. I cannot grace those encounters with the term "romance," however. Habitual routines of sexual expression, begrudgingly or willingly given, in mediocre marriage relationships where the flow of loving is blocked by resentments, disrespectful communications, and discourtesies, cannot be compared to the richness and depth of loving that is experienced in a SoulMate relationship. Rather than frosting being a separate addition as in a literal cake, romance and romantic love-making are the sweet, predictable evolutions of carefully chosen ingredients consistently added to the relationship.

Let's begin with loving touches. Touch alters your brain chemistry by releasing oxytocin and seratonin, hormones that reduce tension, and elevate mood, enhance self-esteem, and strengthen the immune system.

We were on our very first date. We were walking up to a restaurant. Other parties were leaving the restaurant. Jim touched the back of my elbow to steer me through the crowd. That was our first touch, and I instantly knew his skin on mine felt warm and safe to me. A possibility was communicated by that connection. A romantic relationship wouldn't get very far without the touch of skin on skin being pleasurable to both!   I still love Jim's touch. My favorite place to talk things over is with his arm around me, and my head on his shoulder. Whenever we're in a situation where I feel some strangeness or anxiety, his hand in mine or on the small of my back, calms me. I'm not ready for the day unless Jim has spooned me for a few minutes, sleep comes easier if I know he's within touching distance, and my day is better if several loving touches from my SoulMate are scattered throughout it.

---

[77] Davis, Michele Weiner, (2001). <u>The Divorce Remedy</u>, p. 54. New York: Simon & Schuster.

Lisa Collier Cool[78] summarized several major research projects about America's single and married love life. Here are a few of the conclusions from these studies that may surprise you: Married couples have sex more often than singles. Great sex is experienced when you have a strong bond with your mate. Average number of times per month for married couples runs from six to nine. "When asked how sex makes them feel, spouses outscored singles in every measure of delight. Not only are married people the most emotionally fulfilled—they feel loved, wanted, and taken care of while in each other's arms—and they also report high levels of physical pleasure. Far from considering monogamy monotonous, 91 percent of husbands and wives say they aren't just satisfied with their sex lives, they're 'thrilled.' . . .For people who are bonded by love, sex isn't just about the genitals. Sex is about sharing deep feelings, being held, laughing together, allowing each other to lose control, feeling accepted. People who see sex as intercourse only, are more likely to talk about boredom, deception, and distance in their relationships, but those who feel a strong spiritual connection with their partner say that as love and trust build over the years, their sexual relationship grows and grows."

How does all that sound to you? Like more reasons to do the work of integrating all the basic ingredients, spices, and leavening into your relationship?

I find myself reluctant to say some things about our relationship because I know our children, and some day, we hope our grandchildren, will read this book. Why is such a precious, integral part of a loving partnership so hard to discuss with those we love? It *is* private, and should be! What other way do we have of making this very essential part of a loving relationship work, however, if we can't learn from others' successes? So here goes!

As a general rule, women shut down *sexually* whenever experiencing resentment or lack of safety in the relationship. In our "bad" years, I remember telling Jim, "You (a you-message!) can't treat me badly in the family room and expect me to make love to you

---

[78] Cool, Lisa Collier, March, 2001. "Am I Normal?" <u>Good Housekeeping</u>, p. 71-74. New York: Hearst Magazines Division.

in the bedroom!" When resentful or unsafe, many men shut down *emotionally*. I felt left out in the cold, abandoned, when he was emotionally unavailable to me, perpetuating the cycle of my being "out of the mood."

In the days of resentment and fear between us, there were times when I said "no" to love-making because I didn't feel safe . . . I sometimes felt used, rather than loved. You may remember I shared in one of the chapters on co-dependency that we eventually agreed not to do anything for each other that was resented. That agreement included having sex.

When the relationship is safe for both partners and resentments are addressed and dispatched as they arrive, there is no longer resistance to sexual or emotional intimacy. Without those blocks, there is an unobstructed, free flow of love that is expressed as a hug and kiss, an encouraging word, a favor offered, an unpleasant errand run, an apology accepted, understanding given, a practical joke planned and laughed about, a tease, a cuddle, or sexual intercourse. *All* interactions are love-making!

For the past several years there has rarely been even a shadow of resentment between us, therefore, it's also rare for either of us to resist love-making. There *are* times, though, that I do not need or want an orgasm. Most of those times I am happy to offer myself for Jim's pleasure. There is never any hint of feeling used . . . just *being loved* and lov*ing*.

Jim has told me often that he derives more pleasure from my orgasm than from his own! What a magnificent, generous expression of love! Nothing is more reassuring or arousing for him than to have me initiate love-making. More often, however, I sense his loving attention turn toward me and his warm hands on my skin when I have no sexual hunger. When that happens, I think to myself, "I'm too tired for an orgasm, but I'm happy to give him pleasure." After a few minutes of his gentle caresses, though, I find myself responding. He's a persuasive devil! An Italian proverb says, "The bed is the poor man's opera!"

Note: Nearly all of this book was written in 2002 when Book #1 was published. I've actually been surprised by how little I've needed to change or update "Even More" before publishing it. This chapter would be incomplete, however, without the updated information provided by the research of Michelle Weiner Davis, M.S.W. who's book: **The Sex-Starved Marriage: A Couple's Guide to Boosting Their Marital Libido** (2003) and the 2008 sequel, **The Sex-Starved Wife** challenges some of the old assumptions about sexual compatibility and gives practical suggestions to resolve the disparity. Several of my client/couples have found this book very practical and helpful.

Many couples suffer with different levels of sexual desire. Culturally we assume that it's always the man who wants sex more often than the woman, but that isn't always true. A person's unique level of sexual drive is the combination of many genetic, emotional and chemical factors.

If you want the experience of a SoulMate relationship, this mismatch of needs must be resolved. Pat Love (author, speaker, relationship guru) bluntly says how unreasonable it is to expect our partner to be faithful to us and yet be unwilling to meet his or her sexual needs!

Out of love for the higher sexed partner, the partner of lower drive must, at the very least, be willing to be seduced. That means being available at bedtime—not creating chores that keep you from joining your spouse whenever the "time is right." Those of lower drive have found that if they surrender to foreplay, they will often become aroused enough to thoroughly participate in a great expression of love.

Michelle Davis got a group of women together who were very unhappy with their husbands because chores were not done, projects they wanted were not completed. These spouses were treating the needs of their women very lightly! Michelle gave them the assignment of dropping the nagging for one week and during that week try to seduce their husband every day. When the group met again the following week there were multiple stories of chores magically done without further asking and projects completed!

Some of us chuckle at this story. Some may even be offended that sex had to be exchanged for completed projects. My response is that true love gives...and that the journey toward a SoulMate marriage demands that we give whatever is within our power to give in order to meet our loved one's needs. SoulMates even, at times, sacrifice in order to meet the other's need.

This does not mean that one is required to perform sexual acts that feel demeaning or painful or participate in acts that, for you, are immoral. A SoulMate would never demand behaviors of the other that subtracts from love rather than building love and mutual respect.

In closing, there is an ebb and flow to every relationship. It's impossible to be at the peak of romance all of the time! The passion of SoulMates ebbs during times of great adjustment or stress—the birth of a baby, the illness of a child, the death of a parent, or exhaustion from a heavy obligation. But SoulMates are together for the long haul. Patiently, lovingly wait out the ebbs and revel in the flows. You have a lifetime together. Jim and I are both (barely) considered senior citizens by some. We have had countless minor and major ebbs and flows in our 20 years of marriage as well as in our individual lives. Recently we have sensed that we are entering the *real* honeymoon of our lives. We have done the work. *We know the recipe*. We treasure each other and our life together. We are reaping the rewards of all the efforts wc both invested in this relationship. We are eating our Romance Cake every day!

While reading this book, have you felt overwhelmed with all the different "ingredients" to remember? Are you confused about where to begin so you find yourself not beginning anywhere? Here are some suggestions for how to start integrating these romance ingredients into your habit-structure one or two at a time. Read through the suggestions and choose one or two on which you feel ready to work. As a reminder, write them on a sticky note that you move from day to day in your calendar, or buy a hanging calendar and put it inside your medicine cabinet door. Write your choice on the calendar for this month and practice it *every day until it becomes habitual.* Then choose another one or two behaviors from this list, write it at the top of your calendar and practice it *every day until it becomes habitual.* Make a check mark or give yourself a gold star, or, in some way that works for you, put down a physical recognition of each new behavior successfully done. Just *trying* to do it, or *telling* yourself you'll do it doesn't count. It must actually be done and charted on the calendar in order to count as real progress. (Check with your spouse to see if the new behavior is one he or she appreciates. . . it's only beneficial if it is pleasing to your mate!)

One year from now, our bodies will have replaced every current cell with a new one—we'll have a brand new body! If you follow the "one or two new behaviors at a time" regimen, in one year you'll have a brand new marriage, full of romance!

1. Ask your spouse to name three things that, when you do them, warm his or her heart toward you. Write them down on your calendar and begin doing them (Chapter 18 and 19).
2. Ask your spouse for three suggestions for dates that would be romantic for him or her. Make a date to do one of them.
3. Read the Sunday paper with date ideas in mind. Grab a manila folder and begin a file of ideas. Ask your SoulMate for a hot date!
4. Substitute "sometimes" or "rarely" for "always" and "never."
5. Apologize for "you" messages and change them into "I feel . . ." messages.
6. Replace a belief that is not helping to build a SoulMate marriage. The new belief is:

____

7. Get the list of Feeling Vocabulary Words whenever you need to discuss an issue.
8. Perception check when unsure of a message. For example, "I am hearing ___________.
   Is that correct?" (Chapter 5).
9. Complete the quizzes on co-dependency at the end of Chapters 21, 22, and 24.
10. If upset, do the exercise on Identifying and Clearing a Projection (Book #2, Chapter 10).

11. Make a date with your spouse to discuss his or her love language (Book #2, Chapter4).
Take notes and start a file of ways you can express your love in his or her language.
Write down on your calendar each time you follow through and do one of them.
12. Make a list of alternative, healthy ways to vent anger. When angry and about to be disrespectful, excuse yourself and use one of the ways on your list until you are back in control (Book #1, Chapter 12 and 14). Make an appointment with your spouse to mirror the issue and resolve it respectfully (Book #1, Chapter 9).
13. When your spouse is venting about an issue unrelated to your relationship, respond by listening, comforting, and if welcomed, clarifying. Do not try to fix it for him or her (Book #1, Chapter 16).
14. When an issue needs discussing, carefully set the stage (Book #1, Chapter 17) to increase your chances of successful resolution.
15. Commit to the mirroring practice schedule (Book #1, Chapter 9).
16. Make a date for the purpose of brainstorming a list of all the possible fun things you might enjoy doing together on future dates.
17. Acknowledge, praise, or appreciate your partner a minimum of once per day (Book #2, Chapter 5).
18. If you are disrespectful, acknowledge it and apologize immediately. Review with yourself how you will handle a similar situation next time.
19. Say the Commitment to Respect to your partner (Book #1, Chapter 13).

Jim and I guarantee the results of this recipe. It's been laboratory tested by us and by several hundred other couples. There are no shortcuts . . . no packaged mix to be purchased at some romance outlet! When the ingredients are assembled and mixed with love, Romance Cake is the best tasting cake you'll ever eat! It's homemade from scratch and it's worth the effort!

***Puzzle Piece #10: I am gathering and mixing
the ingredients for life-long romance.***

**"Love is not an absolute, a truth, or a limited substance—
that you're in it or out of it.
It's a feeling that ebbs and flows depending on how you
treat each other.
If you learn new ways to interact, the feelings can come
flowing back,
often stronger than before."**
[Sollee, Diane, Director of the Coalition for Marriage, Family
and Couples Education. Interview by Jon Galuckie during a Coalition
conference in Washington, DC in July, 1998.
www.smartmarriage.com.]

**"Sexual intimacy between a man and woman
should be the culmination and expression of the intimacy they
share in *all* areas of their life together.
For sex to be what it is capable of being,
it must be an act of loving and sharing, of
giving to each other."**
[Leman, Dr. Kevin, 2000. Sex Begins in the Kitchen, because
love is an all-day affair. p.11. Grand Rapids, MI: Flemming H.
Revell.]

"Love one another."
I John 2:8

Chapter 15

Ultimate SoulMates: The Last Chapter

"When you realized that every stressful moment you experience is a gift that points you to your own freedom, life becomes very kind."
Byron Katie in *Loving What Is.*

A brief caution before you embark on reading this Last Chapter: It is long. It is deep. You may need to bite it off in small chunks. The beliefs expressed here are decidedly my own. You may agree with them. They may stir up some new thoughts for you to contemplate. You may seriously disagree. But I hope, in the end, you'll have found it thought provoking and exciting and worth the time it took you to work your way through to the end...

ULTIMATE SOULMATES

The title for this chapter was conceived ten years ago when "How to..." and "...Even More" were first written. There has been a blank document with this title sitting on my computer since then. Ten years ago I didn't know how to write the last chapter. I still am not sure how to convey my thoughts...my beliefs...in a clear way, but I know this chapter is the conclusion, perhaps even the frame, for the ten pieces of a SoulMate puzzle. It's been a seed germinating inside of me all of these years. Perhaps it couldn't be written until now...

Recently, for some reason, I've heard several stories of women who were so unhappy in their marriage that they, in great pain and with great regret, left to "find themselves." Then they wrote a best seller about their journey. I have no reason to doubt their story or judge their decisions, but I'm tired of the assumption that happiness can only be found by leaving a troubled relationship or that being unhappy is a good enough reason to leave. Statistically the premise just doesn't hold up. A significantly higher percentage of second and subsequent marriages fail than first marriages. That means that most persons who leave an unhappy first marriage go on to create an unhappy second or subsequent marriage. Statistically, those who leave have a worse chance of finding happiness than those who stay and work it out.

One survey kept track of couples who judged their marriage to be "unhappy." Those who stayed in the marriage, when surveyed five years later, labeled their marriage "happy." Most of those didn't have the benefit of any great intervention. They just stayed until they got through the hard time and were enjoying a better time in their relationship.

In 2005 California Healthy Marriages Coalition, a non-profit, received a ten million dollar grant to be used over five years to teach relationship skills to couples in California in an effort to reduce the divorce rate. For those five years every adult who took an eight hour class filled out an evaluation of their relationship at the beginning of the class, at the end of the class, and again 30 days and six months later. What was discovered was that the most distressed couples made the greatest improvements in their relationships by learning better communication, conflict management and problem solving skills similar to those taught in Book #1. And the couples that learned these skills still showed marked improvement in their relationship six months later—meaning that the benefits lasted over time.

In the counties where the skills classes were most concentrated, a reduction in the divorce rate was documented that could not be accounted for by any other single factor.

These are facts from a strictly sociological perspective. The results for the couples who avoided divorce can be measured in terms of assets saved, depression avoided, children's school and social problems prevented and the burden on society lifted.

ANOTHER POINT OF VIEW

I'd like to look at the lessons learned in marriage from another perspective. Marriage, for me, became my Master Teacher. AS I look back on my life so far, I can appreciate how perfectly the lessons came...many of which are encapsulated in these two " How to..." books.

I must admit however, that I have been a particularly stubborn and slow learner. I've fought my circumstances, been angry, been slow to forgive, slow to accept and not particularly grateful for the painful events that, from the benefit of hind-sight, were the richest treasure troves freom which to mine wisdom.

In spite of my resistance to this classroom, I believe...no, I *know* that there are two parallel realities. The first—the most obvious one—is the physical reality in which we live. Here we experience the realities of life on this planet: childhood, schooling, relationships, jobs, illness, finances—all the stuff that can be summarized or categorized by statistics.

A PARALLEL REALITY

The *other* reality is more elusive for most of us. In that *other* reality we sometimes experience amazing coincidences or synchronicities, have moments of incredible clarity, get insights so wise we know them to have come from outside of our "normal" thoughts. I'm going to label this a spiritual perspective or spiritual reality.

A spiritual perspective is based on the belief that there is a God, a Higher Power, a Universal Intelligence that is grander and wiser than we can imagine. And that this Force is operating on our behalf out of fathomless love for us and a powerful desire for us to experience the best of who we were meant to be. This Spiritual Presence designed each of us with a purpose in mind and *sends* or *allows* (depending on your theology) lessons that if learned, move us toward that purpose for which we were created.

By the time I learned to read at age six and seven, I envisioned myself writing books and speaking in ways that would help others have better relationships. Where did that vision come from? Was that desire borne from the pain I experienced in my family? My longing for my parents to be more loving to each other? Or, did I bring it with me when my soul entered this human experience? Or was I sent to the family that would best germinate the seed of my purpose? I don't know the answer! Just wondering!

LIFE AS A SCHOOL

If you've had much exposure to the spiritual teachings of this age, you have probably heard some version of this statement: "We are spiritual beings have a (temporarily) human experience." And, "Life is a classroom with lessons for my soul." These are often labeled "New Age" but these concepts are deeply rooted in the Christian tradition in which I was reared. The most profound faith is required to believe the well-known scripture from Romans 8:28: "And we know that all that happens to us is working for our good if we love God and are fitting into his plans." [Living Bible.] (I have frequently asked, "All? God, really! All things?") I take that to mean that everything works for my good if I am willing to learn the lessons life brings me. Without cooperating with the lessons, those experiences may just bring fruitless pain. Even that pain, at times, serves to make me more open to different choices, alternate perspectives and will lead to more happiness, less pain.

Although I don't fully understand why certain things have happened to me, I know that everything that has happened brought with it an opportunity for deeper awareness of myself, for growth, for healing, for learning things that have brought priceless value to my life.

I have been a particularly stubborn and slow learner. I haven't relished what a friend calls "another shitty opportunity for growth"! I've fought my circumstances, been angry, been slow to forgive, slow to accept and not particularly grateful for the painful events that, from the benefit of hind-sight, were the richest treasure troves from which to mine wisdom. In other words, do not expect me to be a spiritual teacher!

That said, as I look back on my life so far, I can appreciate how perfectly the lessons came, many of which are encapsulated in these two "How to..." books.

The lens through which I'm asking you to look at creating an Ultimate SoulMate marriage can be applied to any relationship or circumstance. But for now, how does this perspective of life-lessons apply to my relationship to Jim and the amazing SoulMate marriage we built and enjoyed? In a mysterious way that *begins* to be explained by Harville Hendricks Imago Theory. According to that theory, I unconsciously chose Jim as a partner because I knew in my soul that in relationship to him my greatest weaknesses and darkest fears would be exposed for the purpose of my growth and healing. And Jim (unconsciously) chose me as the "teacher" of his next life-lessons. [*Getting the Love you Want* by Harville Hendricks, PhD.]

There's no doubt that we were powerfully, giddily, wildly, wonderfully in love! And naively expected those "in love" feelings to characterize our relationship forever! Yet the life-lessons began the day we returned from our glorious honeymoon. (As is true with most stepfamilies, the honeymoon phase doesn't last very long!) We experienced a small disagreement about how to handle an issue with one of the children. It was the first little tremor that, over the next couple of years, grew into a California sized earthquake opening up a chasm in the ground between us.

CHOICES
Communication, conflict management and problems solving skills are things that can be learned in a classroom or, if you're truly fortunate, absorbed through osmosis while growing up in an amazingly functional and skillful family. Either way, the learning takes place on the human plane...like learning to talk, read, spell or add and subtract. The *choice* of whether or not to learn those skills, or to use them once they have been learned, is a soul choice.

Because we didn't know the communication, conflict management or problem-solving skills to find workable solutions to our differences, our hidden prejudices, judgments, ego trips and capacities for cruelty were brought out into the ugly light of our day-to-day interactions. The negative effect of our lack of skills was multiplied by our poverty of spirit. In other areas, in fact in most areas, we were both kind and generous and giving. Yet in relationship to each other—particularly in regard to the issues over which we disagreed—we were operating from uneducated (human level) and unwilling and unloving (spiritual level) positions.

It often is true that when we as humans make decisions (live life) using a combination of poor life-skills and immature souls, we generate, attract, create, or just simply experience a lot of pain. What if the purpose of that pain is to steer us in a better direction—to stimulate growth on both the practical, earthly plane and the spiritual soul-plane?

Fortunately, and eventually, both Jim and I were willing to learn skills and choose to use them to heal our marriage. I say *eventually* because at first I sought help alone. I was seeing a counselor—learning anger management skills and examining many of my beliefs—for about 2 ½ years before a crisis in our relationship precipitated a choice by Jim to learn with me. I've observed that frequently one partner is willing to start on a learning curve before the other. [Please review Chapter 12, *Won by One*.]

Willingness to seek help was the first step on the spiritual plane. Willingness requires some humility...some awareness that I don't know it all...that I may not be "right"...that there may be skills or principles or changes in belief that will positively improve the relationship.

Soon we were learning new skills—things like speaking in a respectful way (no sarcasm, no tantrums) and listening with the intention to really hear our partner's heart (no more planning what I'm going to say next while Jim was speaking).   [See Book #1.] Those skills are simple enough that a three year old can learn them...and they *do* learn them when those skills are modeled by the adults in their environment! But once learned, then a choice is required to actually *use* them. That is a choice of the spirit—of character—of the soul.

LIGHT BRINGS HEALING

Lara, a woman in one of our early workshops said, "I'm getting the picture that being SoulMates is about being totally, completely transparent with each other." The scripture has been oft quoted and perhaps at times misunderstood, but the truth really does set us free. Truth sheds light on who we are, where the wounds are located, what is needed in order to heal. One of my most respected teachers says that "healing is the application of loving to the place that hurts." Healthy relationships are always reaching for the light, for truth. Every truth is brought out into the light. There are no hidden issues or dark corners. No judgment. No blame. By our acceptance of each other and negotiating workable solutions, loving is being applied to the places that hurt. As we share all we know about ourselves with each other we are bringing the light of heaven to each other and to the earth. Healing takes place. In that process we are transformed into more of who we were meant to be.

In the beginning, I believed that I was using the skills we were learning in order to protect Jim's fragile ego—keep him from getting his feelings hurt. I also, thankfully, saw that our only hope of healing the enormous chasm (wound) between us was by doing something very different than I had been doing. But, in the beginning, using "I statements," avoiding sarcasm, phrasing my communications differently were all just following the instructions I'd been given...like following the instructions to solve an algebra problem. My *willingness* to do these things, in spite of the enormous effort it took to change those patterns, was coming from a soul-place...a deep, hopeful desire that I could be a partner in a truly loving relationship that I had longed for as a child.

It only took a few months of practicing these new skills before I began to notice a kinder, more compassionate, more respectful woman emerging from the ashes of my previous cruelties. Could this painful, agonizing lesson-learning actually be chiseling my higher soul-self from the rough marble boulder of my past self?

I just finished reading "Wild" by Cheryl Strayed in which she documents her amazing physical and spiritual journey while hiking the Pacific Rim Trail. She recounts that Crater Lake (the fourth deepest lake in the US) was once a nearly 12,000 foot high mountain. And then the volcano erupted and its heart was blown apart. The area "was once an empty bowl that took hundreds of years to fill. But hard as I tried, I couldn't see them in my minds' eye. Not the mountain or the wasteland or the empty bowl. They simply were not there anymore. There was only the stillness and silence of that water: what a mountain and a wasteland and an empty bowl turned into after the healing began."

The volcano eruption that nearly emptied out the heart of our marriage took time to heal. The practice of our new skills trickled pure, clean water into the crater of our relationship. Exchange by exchange, one mirroring session at a time, one kept agreement after another, with each kindness given, we slowly filled that crater with pure, healing waters that bathed our wounded spirits and transformed our marriage and us as individuals. The healing of the marriage became the process through which Jim and I emerged as stronger, yet softer, more compassionate human beings.

AN EXPANDED PURPOSE

In 1994 Jim proposed that we teach others the skills that had fashioned for us the SoulMate marriage of our dreams. We had searched for and found from various sources the ten puzzle pieces over about five years. The next layer of soul-fullness was borne as we turned our lessons into a class entitled, *"How to Stay Married & Love It!"* We were discovering a deeper layer purpose as we shared our experience with hundreds of other couples.

Jim began encouraging me to go back to school for my Masters Degree…an endeavor I'd wished for, but been too timid to attempt. I awoke on my 50th birthday knowing that now was the time. As noted elsewhere, he was also encouraging me to turn what we'd learned into a book. It was first published in 2002 and is now re-published as an e-book in 2012 and an audio book in 2015. The *"EVEN MORE"* volume has now been e-published for the first time.

Jim was the source of ecstatic happiness when I "found" him in 1981. And then the source (in combination with my ignorance and willfulness) of excruciating pain. Our journey together led us into the SoulMate relationship for which we had both longed and then led us, unexpectedly, into the soul-work of being of service to others. Could our lessons in loving each other be meant all along to lead to teaching others how to love, as well?

BUT THE STORY DOESN'T END THERE....

We had found and learned the skills we needed. We practiced appreciating each other every day over little and big things. We talked together deeply about our beliefs, our needs, our dreams. We shared our faith and walked the path together that fed our souls. We enjoyed laughter and pleasure, touches and caresses, secret glances across the room that communicated what only we could hear in a crowd. We made love, took vacations, played table games, held grandchildren, saw or spoke on the phone frequently with our children. We held each other through sorrows and listened to each other when one of us was frustrated. We taught classes, struggled with bills, affirmed each other's gifts and contributions to our partnership and the community in which we functioned. When the rare irritation or issue arose (maybe once or twice a year) we immediately began using the skills we'd learned and, usually, it was resolved within five to ten minutes. It felt as though we were making love to each other 24/7 year after year after year. It was heaven on earth!

We dreamed of teaching together for at least the next twenty years—until we were well into our eighties. We had so much of value to share...

A CHANGE OF PLANS

In 2004, immediately following a routine colonoscopy, we were told that Jim had a large mass in his colon. An MRI, CT Scan and surgery quickly followed.   After the surgery, the doctor came to report to me and Jim's daughters that there were large lesions on Jim's liver. The cancer had metastasized. It was advanced enough that the doctor believed he only had a few months to live. Another volcano had erupted in our lives, spreading broken dreams like ashes all over the landscape of our future.

We believed so profoundly that our dreams were truly from God that we rarely wavered in our trust that Jim would be healed. The doctors wanted Jim to embark on chemotherapy in spite of giving us no hope that it would do anything except perhaps extend his life. He said, "No." If he was going to die anyway, he'd rather die without the side effects of chemotherapy. So we changed our diet, went for special holistic treatments, searched high and low for protocols that would help Jim's body triumph over dividing cancer cells.

Most of all we amped up our practice of daily prayers and scripture reading. We kept a journal of what we were reading, what we believed the Holy Spirit was telling us, our feelings, our fears, the test results...everything of any significance was documented in that journal. We believed that it would be the basis of another redemption story like the healing of our marriage.

Although there were moments—or hours—when fear was a consuming monster, for the most part we were quietly going about loving each other, doing what we could and trusting God with Jim's health and our future together.

YOU'VE GOT TO BE KIDDING!

Twice during that year God asked me to surrender Jim to Him— to surrender my agenda that this walk of faith result in Jim's healing. Through many tears, I eventually said, "Thy will be done." It was one of the most agonizing and profound acts of my life.

In about January, 2005 Jim kept getting the message that an event of great significance was going to happen on June 2, 2005. He said, "Something is coming full circle on June 2nd." He "heard" this message several times as we read and prayed together. We had a couple of different explanations of what that might be, but it never occurred to either of us that June 2nd would be the day that Jim's soul would leave his body, ending his time on this physical plane.

THEN...

As those of you know who have been through grief, the depth of my devastation eventually demanded to be acknowledged. It was through my relationship with Jim that I learned and grew and finally experienced the loving relationship for which I had dreamed as a child. It was through Jim's words and tender touches and attitude and hugs and love-making that my fear of being unlovable dissolved. It was in the healing of our marriage that my dream of teaching others how to have happier relationships was realized. It was because of his encouragement that my desire to earn a Masters Degree became a reality. It was due to his unwavering belief in my writing abilities that I eventually held a book written by Nancy Landrum in my hands and saw it listed on Amazon.com! How could he possibly be gone! Could there be anything good left of my life without him?

AND NOW...

A few weeks ago was the seventh anniversary of Jim's passing. The fall-out from this particular volcano is only now beginning to settle. I've been disoriented, angry, withdrawn, exhausted, depressed, hopeless, confused—railing against a God who would so cruelly trick me into believing that He loves me!

I went through one open door, following a faint trail, expecting it to lead to a whole new career for me. It ended in financial ruin.

But I also became certified to teach a program that very closely paralleled what Jim and I had taught together. [*Mastering the Mysteries of Love*. www.skillswork.org.] After years of avoiding anything having to do with stepfamily education, I was invited by the publisher, Mary Ortwein, M.S.W. to join that program with research validated strategies that help stepfamilies succeed. *Mastering the Mysteries of Stepfamilies* was created. Already that program has rescued many stepfamilies from agony of impending divorce as they put into practice the skills and strategies that they learned.

Three of my stepfamily articles were included in an anthology entitled "*All-in-One Marriage Prep: 75 Experts Share Tips and*

Wisdom to Help You Get Ready Now" compiled by Susanne Alexander.

I've taught workshops at national marriage conferences.

I've made significant contributions to the work of the non-profit, California Healthy Marriages Coalition, now known as Healthy Relationships California. [www.RelationshipsCA.org.]

And, amazingly, in spite of a few years of not knowing how the bills would be paid the following month, and experiencing horrendous financial losses, every obligation has been met on time.

I've dreamed of publishing my books as e-books, but knew I needed a huge amount of support from someone far more technologically savvy than I am. This past Spring I *coincidentally* met Carolyn Himes [see her amazing work at www.carolynhimes.com] who says she makes technology friendly to artists who don't know how to promote themselves in this age of "the cloud." She is exactly what I've hoped for and as a bonus, she loves and believes in my work!

Of course, these accomplishments were liberally sprinkled with days of depression, loneliness and longing for my SoulMate. There's been weeks, months, even years of distance and distrust of the God who had so tenderly led us through our life together. There has been an avalanche of questions that seemingly have no answers. And yet there was also grace to keep moving forward.

SPIRITUAL HEALING
While those events might be said to have taken place on the physical level of reality. Here's what's been happening on the spiritual plane:
- My lifelong fear that I can't take care of myself is slowing disappearing.
- I'm gaining confidence in myself as a relationship expert and stepfamily authority.
- I'm beginning to "own" myself as a author, speaker and gifted relationship coach.

- My deep anger and distrust are softening...

These are levels of healing and growth that I'm not sure I would have (or could have) stretched into if Jim were here to lean on. Dare I believe that Jim's SoulMate relationship to me was best served by his death? Can I let down my guard against the next volcano erupting and know that whatever happens is intended for my good? Am I brave enough to embrace the belief that everything that has happened was in service to my higher calling? Can I embrace the Truth that God's love for me has never wavered? And that everything was designed to help me find the Purpose He planned for me from the beginning? Am I willing to open my eyes just a slit and see my life from a spiritual point of view?

After several years of extreme financial struggle, I am just beginning to see the death of that dream as another form of guidance—God saying, "No, Nancy, that's not what I had in mind for you so I'm going to close that door." When I envision that greater Cause behind the horrible decisions I made, the self-judgment falls away and I am more and more often content.

After a lifetime of being afraid that I somehow brought on all the losses in my life because I wasn't good enough or was deserving of punishment, I'm beginning to let the cool, refreshing water of Truth heal the wounds created by those wretched beliefs. The Truth is that I did nothing deserving of pain. I did the best I knew how to do all along, and that path eventually led me to such liberating, life-giving skills that I feel spiritually called—compelled—to share them with others like the woman at the well in John 4:7-30 who's encounter with Jesus was so life-changing that she immediately ran to tell others in her village about him!

When I can (and I can't all of the time!) I view Jim's passing as another expression of his love for me. Wow, that's hard to think, let alone write! I want to argue, "But we'd be so much better together than I am alone! And I still miss him! It still hurts to live without him!" And yet....and yet...maybe, for just a moment, I allow this other spiritual reality in—the possibility that Jim left this earth at exactly the time appointed for him to leave. And that his leaving was a continuation of his love for me in service to my further growth. I look at it. Imagine it. Let its peace spread balm over the wound. Let that viewpoint give me strength to believe in a future for myself that is useful, purposeful, and good.   Until, finally, my purpose is completed and I can leave this challenging classroom behind!

WHAT DOES IT ALL MEAN?

So are you still asking what is meant by Ultimate SoulMates? It means that I embrace the spiritual reality that we are here to serve each other's highest good. It means that when you really tick me off, the school bell is ringing for me. It's time to learn something that, up until now, I haven't known or been willing to learn. Ultimate SoulMates means I'm willing to consider a view much higher than just that your dirty socks on the bathroom floor drive me nuts. It means I stop blaming you for my unhappiness, and look instead for how my own behavior may need to change in order for this relationship to flourish. In circumstances that include abuse or untreated addiction, it may mean leaving the relationship. Even when you have to leave, that partner has served as an Ultimate SoulMate to you, delivering lessons that help you move forward with your soul's purpose.

This is not a path for sissies! This soul-path exposes the worst and leads to the best of who we are meant to be! This soul-path helps us find and be in alignment with our purpose for being on the planet. And this path can be taken with any circumstance, any relationship.

APPLIED TO ANOTHER RELATIONSHIP

I remember a period of time when I was extremely frustrated with my son Steven. A wise Spirit whispered in my ear one day, "The reason you are so angry with him is because he isn't going to change. That means you either live in a state of anger with him or do something very different than you are doing now." I thought through what would have to happen to take the anger out of my relationship to him. I made some changes. The anger magically disappeared. It wasn't his "fault" after all. He was giving me a wonderful opportunity to learn and grow new skills...to understand our dynamics from a different point of view.

THE PAYOFF

As I look back on the events in my life that delivered what seemed to be catastrophic volcano-like eruptions, I realize that the learnings, the beliefs, the perspectives, the skills that I value the most have come as those eruptions called me to learn and grow in ways that I never would have chosen for myself. Everything I write about and teach that others find helpful comes from those events that at first glance (first 1000 glances!) seemed like the most horrible tragedies. Didn't God know who I was? I was a nice Christian woman! This stuff wasn't supposed to happen to me. Why didn't he protect me from this pain?

Yet, perhaps this Loving Presence, so constant in my life, was using these events to fulfill my deepest desires and accomplish His purpose for me in this lifetime.

Please don't misunderstand me. I don't' want any more volcanic eruptions! I've heard some spiritual giants say that it's possible to learn and grow without the stimulus of pain. I'm sick of pain! I sincerely hope the hard lessons are behind me. But, at least in my past, nearly all—if not all—of the growth I've experienced has been motivated by wanting to get out of pain. Maybe, (please?) can I learn now from a place of trust and stability?

All I can say for certain is that it is my intention, while remaining very human and allowing myself my human reactions to anything that brings pain, to also view what I can see through the lens of the spirit. I intend to spent far more time being grateful for all that Jim taught me—both by his life and in his death—and much less time regretting the extended time with him that I was denied.

Most of you don't know me, so you don't realize what a monumental act of courage it is for me to think these thoughts, expose these beliefs and write out these intentions! Earlier this year I sensed that this was going to be a year that called for courage. So I got out my poster paints and painted the word COURAGE in bright lime green on a yellow background and with a big red arrow moving diagonally up across the page and a few little bouquets of flowers perched here and there. I put it in an old frame. It's hanging where I can see it now and look at it often.

This is copied from my journal a few years ago: "I've been listening to a book on tape: *The Soul's Religion* by Thomas Moore. Thoughts: We spend so much of our physical lives trying to figure things out...prove things...like my quest to understand how loving relationships work... but the life of faith is a life of unknowing...of jumping off a cliff. The spiritual walk is a journey of mystery that has to start with a humility of heart that comes from being stripped of our ego strengths or weaknesses... even my fear of moving out into the world is a protection of ego and it gets in the way of experiencing God plan for me. While listening I was reminded again of the parallel paths...physical and spiritual. The more I am aware of the spiritual path, the less the physical path upsets me or excites me."

I am being very bold to suggest that you join the growing legion of human beings who are accepting the challenge of seeing life as the school where lessons are custom designed for our soul's growth. Give it some thought. What if his work-aholism (or procrastination or ...?) is your call to growth? What if her unhappiness (or over-spending or....?) is your invitation to a higher level of loving? What if your child's misbehavior is the perfect magnet that will attract you to a new way of parenting? What if this illness is heaven sent?

"SO," YOU ASK, "HOW DO I BEGIN?"

Buy a spiral notebook or a fancy journal or open a file on your computer titled "Gratitude." I know of no more powerful way to begin than to start deliberately, purposefully and frequently *expressing gratitude for the very things that seem to be the cause of your pain.* Can there be any greater expression of faith in the ultimate goodness of the Universe's benevolent plan for you than to be grateful *before* you see the answers? Sarah Ban Breathnoch's book *Simple Abundance* launched many of us on the spiritual practice of keeping a gratitude journal in the '90s. Oprah Winfrey still states that writing down five things for which you are grateful every day for four months will change your life forever. I'm asking you to take it a step further by being grateful not only for the simple pleasures in your life that you may be taking for granted, but adding gratitude for the hard things for which you can't yet see a purpose. You may even find yourself noticing positive things about this person, relationship or circumstance that have been previously overlooked due to your focus on unhappiness.

Gratitude *before* you see the blessing will stir things up in the spiritual world! It will say to the Universe, I'm ready to work with you on finding the blessing in this relationship or circumstance!" It opens up a lace in your heart and your mind for steps to be identified, for new strategies to be tried, for magical "coincidences: to happen that will bring you exactly what you need to move forward. Bishop T.D.Jakes from The Potter's Wheel church in Dalls, TX reminds us that Jesus blessed what was *not enough* (five loaves and two fishes for a crowd of 500 hungry guests) before it could be transformed into *more than enough* (12 baskets left over)!

The practice of Gratitude also humbles us. It softens a hard place inside that, in the past, has insisted on blaming another for the pain. Gratitude helps me acknowledge that there may be solutions that I haven't been ready to see or behaviors that may bring love and healing that I've been too proud to try. Being grateful for what is currently a challenge also puts me on the alert so that I am actively, trustingly waiting to notice a clue from a song, or a phrase someone says or pick up a book I wouldn't have given a second glance to before or see an ad for a class or go online and search for resources. It's announcing to the spiritual realm, "Bring it on! I'm ready to change! Just tell me what to do!" Then keep it up! Refuse to give up! Some answers take a while to arrive! But *when* they arrive, they are sweeter and more precious than anything else you can imagine!

And remember, that what you are led to do may require all the strength and courage you can muster to put into practice. You can do whatever it takes. That was a "given" the moment you chose to open the door to this path with your gratitude! *Every* human being ever born has the capacity to walk this spiritual path successfully! The ability is part of our spiritual DNA!

It's also important for me to point out that expressing Gratitude is an act of the will...an act of faith. It doesn't require that you always *feel* grateful in order for it to work.

DO YOU REALLY DO THIS?

You have every right to ask, "Do you practice what you're asking me to do?" Jim and I expressed gratitude for his illness, trusting that there was some Wisdom behind this unwanted and unexpected circumstance. We also had times of confessing our fears—to each other and to God. There had been many other circumstances on our journey together and separately for which we expressed thanks, not knowing what possible good would emerge, but trusting in the power of gratitude and the ultimate Goodness that guided our lives.

Immediately following his death, by an act of will, I said, "God, thank you for Jim's death. I don't understand it. I don't want it. I can't see any good that can come from it, but by faith, I thank you." In the following years, I confess I rarely said "thank you" for being left on my own, but continued to practice what I consider a spiritual discipline of gratitude in regard to other things. As expressed earlier in this chapter, I've recently considered a deeper, more profound purpose for Jim's death.

In the past several months I've been going through another major transition. I've felt a strong pull toward publishing my books as e-books and eventually writing the book for stepfamilies that has been germinating in my heart for the past five years. While this pull has been growing I've had some major health challenges that ultimately led to my asking for a leave of absence from my job in spite of needing that income. During the months that these things have been developing I've been pondering how to pray. Do I pray for successful books? Do I ask God for healing? Do I look at my meager savings and, at an age when many people retire, quit my job and begin paying for an internet coach? If I pursue this path am I being foolish or guided to a higher purpose?

I finally decided that I can ask for whatever I want, but at the end of every prayer, I add, "Thy will be done," a statement of understanding that I don't always know what is best for me but I can trust the Universal Intelligence that sees all, knows all, and will powerfully act on my behalf to bring about the best. So every morning I wake up and say, "Thy will be done in me today. Thy will be done through me today. No matter what happens—whether I putter in the yard, take an afternoon nap, coach a couple needing support or write an article for a national magazine—I trust you to know and do for me what is best."

After praying that prayer one recent morning, I spent several hours with Carolyn working on formatting for the publishing of "How to..." On the way home traffic came to a sudden stop and though I slammed on my brakes, I could see the large utility van in my rear view mirror was not go ing to stop. It crashed into my car's trunk and plowed through until my driver's seat was shoved forward and my head thrown sideways and forward so my forehead shoved the radio into the dash. As things became quiet, I realized my head was bleeding so I grabbed something to blot the blood. And then, before anyone reached me, I said, "Thank you, God. I trust you have a good reason for this accident."

When the paramedics arrived, although extremely shaken, I was able to get out of the car on my own, lay on the gurney to be taken to the ER to have my head and both wrists x-rayed. I didn't see my car until the next day when I went to the wrecking yard to collect my personal items. If you saw the photos you'd be amazed that I escaped with only scrapes and bruises.

Over the next few days gratitude couldn't be found on my lips or in my heart. My fully paid for six year old car with 130,000 miles on it was totaled. At a time when I needed every penny, I was paying for extra chiropractor's appointments to straighten out my twisted back and sore neck and shoulder. My energy level was lower than ever. I felt frustrated and angry and not at all grateful!

Yet within a few weeks, the insurance company paid far more than I was expecting for my totaled car. I put some of the money in the bank and the rest down on a new-used car with only 19,000 miles on it, a full, 7-year factory warranty and low payments I can afford. My doctor bills were ultimately paid by the other driver's insurance. My bruises healed and I had more money in the bank than before the accident to finance this launching of my e-books.

Do I know how it's all going to turn out? Am I sure the books will help enough people and sell well enough to support me? No, and no. I only know I am moving forward one step at a time, making the best decisions I can, following the strong urgings of what I believe to be Guidance within me.

I'm not a spiritual giant, and I'm not as consistently grateful or trusting as I wish I were.   I struggle, but yes, I practice what I am asking you to do...

IN CONCLUSION

I hope you accept the challenge. I suspect you were already heading this way or you wouldn't have completed reading this chapter! You might have deleted this book from your I-Pad or Kindle by now! I welcome fellow travelers on this path! And crave for you the deep soul-satisfaction of knowing that you are more of the wise, loving being you were intended to be—bringing healing and love to yourself and into your world in whatever ways you are led—because you've chosen the path of Ultimate SoulMates!

I welcome you to my website: www.nancylandrum.com or go to http://www.facebook.com/NancyLandrumAuthorCoach and let me know how this soul-path is working for you! I am eager to provide support and encouragement!

"In everything give thanks."
Ephesians 5:20

MORE RESOURCES

Note from Nancy: It is impossible to get different results without changing what *you* do.   Without making changes in your own behavior, it is fruitless to expect anything—including other persons— to change or ultimately, the relationship to change. I cannot think of one personal example of another person changing without also changing myself.   It's easy to blame someone else for the current state of your relationship, whether a spouse or a child.   But the result is to perpetuate the pain.   Blame is wasted energy that only keeps us stuck where we are.   Please take advantage of these additional resources to help you identify ways *you* can change your contributions to the relationship!

ADDITIONAL OFFERINGS BY NANCY:

On Nancy's website you can subscribe to her newsletter, investigate all of her offerings, contact Nancy, or enroll in her private coaching program. Nancylandrum.com

How to Stay Married & Love It! Solving the Puzzle of a SoulMate Marriage, 2002. Thoroughly covers the first four corner pieces of the SoulMate puzzle, the practices that were foundational as Jim and Nancy saved their floundering marriage. Some have said this book reads like a novel!

The **Millionaire Marriage Club**, an online relationship skills course delivered in 19 half-hour lessons covering eight major areas of a healthy marriage. Enroll at www.nancylandrum.com

The **Millionaire Marriage Club** *mini-courses*. The full length MMC is divided into mini-courses covering topics like Communication, Loving and Feeling Loved, Conflict Management, and Beliefs. Enroll at www.nancylandrum.com

Stepping TwoGether: Building a Strong Stepfamily (2020) Combining the personal stories of several step-couples as well as the Landrum's with research validated strategies that are characteristic of most stepfamilies who are successfully thriving.

The **Love Potions for Healthy Relationships Series** delivers the same communication and conflict management skills taught in the How to… books but with illustrations from other relationships such as parent to child, friend to friend, boss to employee, co-workers. Etc. These are pithy, small, easy-to-read books that target specific aspects of a healthy relationship.

Includes:

Season the Pot: an explanation of how our unconscious beliefs influence the relationships we choose or create and how to exchange poor beliefs for more functional ones in order to get a better result.

Communication Elixers: The same powerful communication skills from How to Stay Married & Love It! with practical illustrations from relationships other than a marriage.

Savory Safeguards: The recipe for managing powerful emotions like anger, bitterness, and fear that, untreated, pollute the physical and emotional health as well as relationships.

Pungent Boundaries: If you're tired of feeling resentful and taken advantage of, this little gem is for you!   An explanation of codependency that you can understand and relate to, as well as directions for setting healthy boundaries and enforcing consequences that will set you free.

Other Authors I Recommend:

Chapman, Gary. (December, 1992).   <u>The Five Love Languages</u>. Chicago: Moody Press. This is a great guide for discovering why certain actions make you feel loved, while your spouse may need different actions from you in order to feel loved.
misunderstanding of what it means to love someone unconditionally.

Davis, Michele Weiner, (2001).   <u>The Divorce Remedy, The Proven 7-Step Program for Saving Your Marriage.</u> New York: Simon & Schuster. This book is the sequel to her best seller, Divorce Busting, in which she has refined and clarified the principles that have helped thousands save their marriages. It is written in a personable and conversational style. She proposes solutions to locked-in problems that are refreshing, supremely practical, and that work! It isn't necessary to be on the brink of divorce in order to benefit from her "do what works" plan.

Davis, Michele Weiner website: www.divorcebusting.com. Browse through Michele's amazing array of relationship books and products including: Divorce Busting and The Sex Starved Marriage.

Harley, Dr. Willard F. Jr., (1992). <u>Love Busters</u>. Grand Rapids, Michigan: Flemming H. Revell Publishers. Dr. Harley identifies the five most common habits that destroy romantic love and teaches how to eliminate them once and for all. (7th Printing, 2000). 5 Steps to Romantic Love: A Workbook for Readers of Love Busters and His Needs, Her Needs. Grand Rapids, MI: Flemming H. Revell. www.marriagebuilders.com.

Hendricks, Gay & Kathlyn, (1992). <u>Conscious Loving: the Journey to Co-commitment, a Way to be Together Without Giving up Yourself</u>. New York: Bantam Books. The personal example of their own marriage makes this call to deeper intimacy and healing especially powerful. A great resource for advanced relationship work. (Feb. 1999). The Conscious Heart: 7 Soul Choices That Inspire Creative Partnership. New York: Bantam Books. www.hendricks.com.

Hendrix, Harville, (1990). <u>Getting the Love You Want</u>, New York, NY: Harper & Row, Publishers, Inc. This book is rich with exercises that, by the time we completed them, gave us profound appreciation for the inner wisdom that brought us together. He and his wife Helen Hunt have also written a relationship course called "Couplehood." Explore his products at www.HarvilleHendrix.com.

Nichols, Michael P., Ph.D., (1995). <u>The Lost Art of Listening</u>. New York: Guilford Press. The entire book is about the importance of listening to the process of real communication. He explores why it is hard to listen, and the benefits to all relationships if listening skills are improved. The book is full of pithy little nuggets of listening truth, which is why I quote him so often. Also, Stop Arguing with Your Kids: How to Win the Battle of Wills by Making Your Kids Feel Heard. Go to www.Amazon.com.

Waite, Linda J., and Maggie Gallagher, (September, 2000). <u>The Case for Marriage: Why Married People Are Happier, Healthier, and Better Off Financially</u>. New York: Random House. This authoritative and provocative book reveals the benefits—emotional, physical, economic, and sexual—that marriage brings to individuals and society. This book is summarized in **How to Stay Married & Love It!** Chapter 18.

ADDITIONAL MARRIAGE SUPPORT WEB SITES:

www.smartmarriages.com. Diane Sollee, who hosts this site, is director, and founder of the Coalition for Marriage, Family and Couples Education. The Coalition serves as an information clearinghouse on skills-based marriage education. If you get on her e-mail list, you will receive a wealth of the most current articles, research, news, and legislation in the field of marriage and family welfare.

www.virginia.edu/marriageproject. "The National Marriage Project's purpose is to strengthen the institution of marriage by providing research and analysis that informs public policy, educates the American public, and focuses attention on a problem of enormous scope and consequence. Simply stated, marriage is declining as an institution for childbearing and child rearing, with devastating consequences for millions of children." Co-directed by Barbara Dafoe Whitehead, Ph.D.,and David Popenoe, Ph.D.

APPLYING THE PRINCIPLES of "How to Stay Married & Love It!" TO CHILD-REARING:

Chapman, Gary, (1997). <u>The Five Love Languages of Children</u>. Chicago: Northfield Publishing. (2000). The Five Love Languages of Teenagers. Chicago: Northfield Publishing. These books teach us how to identify the primary way that each child receives the message, "I am loved." These are enormously helpful concepts to make sure that the love we feel for our children is being communicated in a way that is easiest for each child to receive.

Major, Jayne A., Ph.D., (2000). <u>Breakthrough Parenting</u>: Quality Publishing. This book shows you how to: Discipline effectively, promoting willing cooperation from your children. Set appropriate and clear boundaries together with your children. Turn mistakes into positive learning experiences. Promote confidence and healthy self-esteem. Communicate so that everyone listens and understands. Help all family members accept personal responsibility for their actions. Resolve conflicts quickly and easily with win-win methods. Form a deep and lasting bond with your children. It can be ordered from Amazon.com or directly from www.Breakthroughparenting.com.

Sprague, Gary, with Randy Petersen, (1993). <u>Kid's Hope</u>. Colorado Springs: CO: Thomas Nelson Publishers. This book comes in different versions appropriate for different ages. These books are great for the biological parent (in the case of blending families) to go through with the child as a vehicle for helping the child talk about feelings. They are also appropriate for single parents, and a divorced or widowed parent.

MORE FOR STEPFAMILIES:

<u>National Stepfamily Resource Center</u>: serves as a clearing house of information linking family science research on stepfamilies and best practices. www.stepfamilies.info.

Deal, Ron, M.MFT. <u>Building a Successful Stepfamily</u>, Audio Seminar. Nine hours of presentation on six CDs plus a 98 page seminar manual has over 150 practical ideas for strengthening your stepfamily. This set may be purchased at www.swfamily.org/stepfamily. It is particularly geared toward Christians. www. SmartStepfamilies.com.

Houck, Don and LaDean Houck, (1997). <u>The Ex Factor: Dealing with Your Former Spouse.</u> Grand Rapids, MI: Flemming H. Revell.   An excellent resource for learning how to successfully work with an ex-spouse.

DIVORCE INFORMATION:

Melved, Ph.D., 1989). <u>The Case Against Divorce</u>. Discover the lures, the lies, and the emotional traps of divorce—plus the seven vital reasons to stay together. New York: Ballantine Books. Winner of the 1990 Christopher Award.

Wallerstein, Judith, Julia Lewis, & Sandra Blakeslee, (2000). <u>The Unexpected Legacy of Divorce: A 25 Year Landmark Study</u>. New York: Hyperion. In depth interviews of 131 children every five years beginning 25 years ago after the divorces of their parents. Interviews with children with parallel lives who's happy or conflict ridden parents chose to stay together provide accurate contrast to the long-term effects of divorce into middle adulthood.

FOR CHILDREN OF DIVORCE:

Major, Dr. Jayne A. <u>Creating a Successful Parenting Plan, a Step-be-Step Guide for the Care of Children of Divided Families.</u> Steven A. Mindel, a Family Law Attorney,   says about this book, "Finally someone has prepared a practical guide to   developing a parenting plan which takes into account both the emotional and legal aspects of child custody and visitation." Deanie Kramer, a divorce mediator   adds, "Parents working together to create a parenting plan are 80% more   successful in carrying out the plan than when a third party, who does not know the family, dictates what they should be doing." This book may be ordered from   Breakthrough Parenting, Inc.1-800-770-7935 or www.breakthroughparenting.com.

Rothchild, Gillian, (1999). <u>Dear Mom and Dad: What Kids of Divorce Really Want to Say to Their Parents</u>. New York: Pocket Books. 180

pithy words of advice from children to their parents who have
divorced.